A GUIDE TO WRITING SOCIOLOGY PAPERS

FOURTH EDITION

THE SOCIOLOGY WRITING GROUP

Coordinators and Editors
Judith Richlin-Klonsky and Ellen Strenski

AUTHORS
Roseann Giarrusso
Judith Richlin-Klonsky
William G. Roy
Ellen Strenski

ST. MARTIN'S PRESS
New York

Editor in chief: Steve Debow
Development editor: Anne Dempsey
Managing editor: Patricia Mansfield Phelan
Project editor: Diana M. Puglisi
Production supervisor: Kurt Nelson
Art director: Lucy Krikorian
Cover and text designer: Evelyn Horovicz

Library of Congress Catalog Card Number: 97-65377

Manufactured in the United States of America.

3 2 1 0 9 8
f e d c b

For information, write:
Worth Publishers
33 Irving Place
New York, NY 10003

www.worthpublishers.com

ISBN: 0-312-13762-1

CONTENTS

TO THE INSTRUCTOR

A *Guide to Writing Sociology Papers* has been extremely well received by instructors in a wide range of sociology courses since the publication of the First Edition. Both instructors and countless students have benefited from its clear, straightforward, and engaging style. In this Fourth Edition, we have added information that demonstrates our commitment to new technology as a valuable tool in sociology writing. This added focus serves to strengthen our original message.

The quality of student writing is a constant concern to college teachers. Like their colleagues in other disciplines, many sociology instructors, preoccupied by the demands of their profession and dreading the likelihood of poorly written or perhaps plagiarized papers, despair of assigning writing and rely instead on tests. But to do so deprives students of the active, personal engagement with sociological concepts and data that only writing about them can provide. This book is an attempt to do something about this problem.

FLEXIBLE DESIGN

A *Guide to Writing Sociology Papers* grew out of our collective experiences as sociology and English faculty members, teaching assistants, counselors, and tutors at UCLA. The book is designed to relieve you of some of the burden of writing instruction and to provide your students—from beginning to advanced—with practical advice. Its format is flexible enough to accommodate specific modifications, yet "spelled out" enough to guide those who need to pay special attention to all steps in the writing process, from initial conceptualization to final presentation.

WRITING AS EXERCISING THE SOCIOLOGICAL IMAGINATION

The underlying premise of the book is that thinking and writing are integrally related, and, therefore, that writing a sociology paper involves exercising the "sociological imagination." Throughout the book, our advice and examples are informed by this practical pedagogical observation. When instructors comment to students that their papers "are too psychological" or "really don't address a sociological issue," for example, students tend to be confused and rarely learn how to correct the problem in later papers. Similarly, comments that a paper "has no structure," "follows no clear logic," or "lacks sufficient evidence" often baffle students. Our goal here is to provide both you and your students with illustrations and a common language for discussing and improving papers in these areas.

vi

ACCESSIBILITY TO STUDENTS

The book can be used in a variety of ways in both lower- and upper-division sociology courses. For example, you can assign it as a reference tool for students to consult on their own. Or you can refer in class or in discussion sections to specific parts when you mention papers, explaining how students can apply our advice to your assignment and how our sample student papers do or do not represent what you expect. Or, in your comments on drafts or in individual conferences with students, you can refer students to specific pages in the text.

In addition, the book can be used in a range of writing classes from remedial to advanced. It is especially appropriate for adjunct writing courses paired with sociology courses. However, since much of the advice we present can be generalized to other disciplines, the book is also suitable as a basic text in advanced writing courses that emphasize the social sciences. Much of the book—Chapters 2, 3, 5, 6, 7, and Part III—applies equally to courses in the humanities.

STUDENT-FRIENDLY WRITING STYLE

While we focus on the priorities most commonly identified by instructors, our own writing style is intentionally "student-friendly." Students report that learning about writing is sometimes boring or intimidating. Thus, our tone is deliberately easygoing, avoiding prohibitions where possible, including contractions where they soften the prose, and offering guidelines rather than commandments. We also include many concrete examples, some taken from student papers, to make the guidelines less abstract.

A NOTE ABOUT THE FOURTH EDITION

Several new features make the Fourth Edition of *A Guide to Writing Sociology Papers* an up-to-date and useful tool for students and instructors alike. Reflecting the field's movement toward greater theoretical diversity, for instance, we have revised Part I, "Essentials," to include detailed information about the range of sociological paradigms, theories, and methods. In addition, the Fourth Edition includes new material on electronic communication and research as well as expanded discussions of plagiarism and techniques for revision.

▶ **Electronic Communication and Research.** Part II, "Writing from Various Data Sources," has been updated to reflect the growing use of electronic communication in sociological research. The introduction to Part II incorporates several new sections on locating online information, searching for online information with Boolean operators, and evaluating Internet information. It also includes a list of Web sites relevant to sociologists, as well as advice on how to sift through the often overwhelming amount of electronic information that is available on the Internet. In addition, we have included more "computer tips" throughout the text, updated the lists of specialized sociological references to include many more electronic databases, and expanded the list of scholarly journals that can help students develop creative research questions and locate relevant empirical studies.

▶ **Plagiarism and Revision.** In the sections on revision and on plagiarism in Chapters 3 and 4 we have incorporated more detailed instructions and more examples of what to do (and what not to do), in order to help students avoid the pitfalls associated with referencing scholarly works. Because revision is among the most difficult steps in the writing process, we have aimed to provide students with useful techniques for improving their sociological writing.

Acknowledgments

We thank Jeffrey Alexander, Melvin Pollner, and Geraldine Moyle, all at UCLA, for their help in locating appropriate student papers. Special thanks go to the student authors—Lysa Agundez, Alvin Hasegawa, Tiffany Seden, and Daryl Williams—for their permission to use their work as examples.

Alice M. Roy, Coordinator of the Writing Program at California State University, Los Angeles, made helpful suggestions on the "Developing an Argument: Logic and Structure" section in the first chapter. Several colleagues provided valuable comments on earlier drafts of portions of Part II: Robert M. Emerson and Linda L. Shaw ("The Ethnographic Field Research Paper"), and Kenneth Bailey and Gina Randolph ("The Quantitative Research Paper"). Professor Emerson also generously granted permission to adapt sections of the guidelines on ethnographic field research he distributes to his students. In addition, we would like to thank Mary Jo Johnson, Undergraduate Counselor in UCLA's Department of Sociology, for her encouragement of this project and unwavering support of enhanced undergraduate education. Profound thanks are also due to Constance Coiner, Arlene Dallalfar, Lisa Frohmann, and Nancy A. Matthews, contributors to previous editions of *A Guide to Writing Sociology Papers*.

We would like to acknowledge our gratitude to the following professors who assisted in the revision of this book by responding to our questions about the previous edition: David K. Brown, University of Wisconsin–Eau Claire; Charles Cappell, Northern Illinois University; MariJean Ferguson, La Roche College; Jill S. Grigsby, Pomona College; Robert Liebman, Portland State University; Kathleen McKinney, Illinois State University; Elizabeth J. Mitchell, Bucknell University; Arthur E. Paris, Syracuse University; Rachel Parker-Gwin, Virginia Tech; Clifford L. Staples, University of North Dakota; Donald E. Stull, The University of Akron; and Donald L. Yates, Oklahoma State University. We are also grateful to development editor Anne Dempsey and project editor Diana Puglisi, at St. Martin's Press, for all their help in preparing the fourth edition.

A *Guide to Writing Sociology Papers* continues the commitment to teaching of our friend and colleague Constance Coiner (1948–1996), who contributed in a major way to the first edition of this book. The pages of this Fourth Edition reflect both her devotion to students and her dedication to pursuing clarity of thought and expression as a means of effecting political change.

ABOUT THE AUTHORS

The members of the Sociology Writing Group came together in 1984 to prepare a guide for instructors and students in sociology and writing courses at UCLA. *A Guide to Writing Sociology Papers* grew out of this collaborative effort. Judith Richlin-Klonsky and Ellen Strenski coordinated the group's work and edited the book.

Roseann Giarrusso is Research Assistant Professor of Sociology and Gerontology at the University of Southern California (USC). She is also Project Director of USC's ongoing Longitudinal Study of Four-Generation Families, which has followed over 300 multigenerational families for more than twenty-six years. Her research interests include intergenerational family relations, social psychology, and the sociology of aging, the life-course, and gender. Holding an M.A. and Ph.D. in sociology from UCLA, and an M.A. in psychology, she has taught courses in both fields and has conducted workshops at universities throughout Southern California on how to succeed in college. Roseann Giarrusso's contributions to the book include Chapter 9, major portions of Chapters 2 and 3, and the list of sociology-related journals in Chapter 7.

Judith Richlin-Klonsky is Lecturer in Sociology at UCLA, where she has taught courses in the sociology of everyday life, medical sociology, and the sociology of age, mental illness, and group processes. She has also brought a sociological perspective to editing projects in a variety of fields. She holds a master's degree in family therapy and received her Ph.D. in sociology from UCLA, where she was trained in qualitative research methods and an interpretive theoretical framework. Her recent research publications include an analysis of the history of the marriage and family therapy license in California and a longitudinal case study of a five-generation family. Judith Richlin-Klonsky's contributions to the book include Chapter 8 as well as major portions of Chapters 1 and 6.

William G. Roy is Professor of Sociology at UCLA, winner of the 1989 Luckman Award for Distinguished Teaching, and author of *Socializing Capital: The Rise of the Large Industrial Corporation in America* (Princeton University Press, 1997). He specializes in comparative-historical sociology, particularly long-term political and economic transformations. William G. Roy contributed to the overall development of Chapter 1 and wrote the Framing a Question and the Developing an Argument: Logic and Structure sections in that chapter. He also contributed to Chapter 6 and to the Locating Specialized Sociological References section in Chapter 7.

Ellen Strenski is Assistant Writing Director in the Department of English and Comparative Literature at the University of California at Irvine. In addition to coauthoring *The Research Paper Workbook* (New York: Longman, 3rd ed., 1991) and *Making Connections across the Curriculum: Readings for Analysis* (Boston: Bedford, 1986), she has published articles in many pedagogical journals on the subject of writing in diverse disciplines. Most recently, she has exercised her sociological imagination in several articles and chapters that analyze issues in writing program administration. Ellen Strenski's contributions to the book include Chapter 4; major portions of Chapters 3, 5, and 7; and the tips on locating and assessing online information in Part II. She also contributed to Chapters 1 and 6.

TO THE STUDENT

If you're uneasy about the prospect of writing a sociology paper, you're not alone. Many students feel as you do; that's why we wrote this book. We can't promise that your assignment will be easy, but it *can* be done, and done well. This book can help you feel in control of the writing process from beginning to end, and it can help you produce your best work.

We've written the guide we wish we'd had as undergraduates. We learned too late what "explicate" means. We didn't know how to include our field notes. We had to return to the library at the last minute to find page numbers for passages we needed to cite because we neglected to jot them down in the first place, and we experienced many other problems in writing our own papers. We want to spare you some of the trouble we endured. And we have learned that procrastination—our own and that of others—is not always the result of laziness but often a sign of uncertainty about just how to begin and complete a given writing task.

WHAT YOUR INSTRUCTOR EXPECTS

Our students often tell us that they don't know what they're expected to do in a paper or that they don't know what the instructor wants. So we've tried to demystify the whole process. For example, we explain in Chapter 1 what makes a sociology paper different from papers in other disciplines and what sociology instructors want in terms of a paper's logic and structure. We suggest ways to get started and to stay on track, ways to deal with and present your data, ways to troubleshoot your writing, and ways to make your prose look and sound professional. All along the way our book gives practical illustrations, including sample student papers that you can compare with your own. These sample papers are very good but they are not perfect. We comment on their fine features and suggest alternatives where problems remain.

We recommend that everyone read Part I, "Essentials," and Part III, "Finishing Up." The chapters in Part II, "Writing from Various Data Sources," can be used selectively. Use the table of contents and the index to look up what you need.

GETTING STARTED

Chapter 1 focuses on the conceptual starting points that are fundamental for writing a good sociology paper. Chapters 2, 3, 4, and 5, respectively, present basic guidelines on organizing your time; writing and revising; keeping track of citations, notes (especially for electronic sources), and references to avoid plagiarism; and polishing your paper. Follow these guidelines from the beginning of your project.

DOING YOUR RESEARCH AND WRITING IT UP

Treat Part II, "Writing from Various Data Sources," as a reference tool. Read the introduction, which gives you an overview of and offers tips on locating and evaluating information from electronic databases. Then, delve into the individual chapters as you need them. The chapters in Part II cover four typical kinds of sociology papers that are, in turn, based on four different data sources: the textual analysis paper (Chapter 6), the library research paper (Chapter 7), the ethnographic field research paper (Chapter 8), and the quantitative research paper (Chapter 9). The chapter on library research includes a list of specialized sociological reference sources. The other three chapters contain student papers as illustrations.

Part III, "Finishing Up," includes a checklist for your final draft and suggestions for expanding your sociological imagination.

HOW TO USE THIS BOOK

Don't try to read the whole book at one go. Chapter 2 and the four chapters in Part II are meant to guide you through steps in a process. Use these chapters as you would instructions for assembling anything—first scan the chapter to get a sense of what you're in for and then consult it carefully as you move along step by step. Sometimes a writing assignment can loom as an enormous, mysterious undertaking because students don't know how to break it down into smaller, more manageable tasks. This guide does that for you. There may be portions of the guide that you'll have to reread before they make sense to you, and other portions that you'll refer to again and again for present and future writing assignments.

The primary purpose of this book is to help you prepare good sociology papers, and, except for Chapter 9 on quantitative research, which is more technical than the other chapters, you'll be able to use this book from day one of any sociology course. But you'll also find that much of this book applies as well to other social sciences, and that many parts will even help you write papers in the humanities. *A Guide to Writing Sociology Papers* will help you from the start to the finish of your college career.

OTHER SUGGESTIONS

Your own campus may offer other resources to help you further.

- Find out if your campus library offers a tour so that you can get an overview of its organization. A short time invested at the beginning of the quarter or semester when schedules tend to be less demanding may save you many hours of wandering and wondering later.

- Find out if your English department offers composition courses in which you can practice and develop writing skills. Investigate writing courses even if you have fulfilled the requirement for basic English composition. (Don't let English majors corner the market on intermediate or advanced courses.) At some colleges special writing courses are attached to sociology and other courses, a combination that benefits you doubly. If you are concerned that your present writing skills might earn a less-than-satisfactory grade in a composition class, check out the possibility of taking the course as an elective on a pass/no-pass basis.
- Find out if your campus has a tutoring center where peer or professional tutors can review your work with you and help you strengthen your writing skills.

A Note on Our Writing Style

Before going on, we would like you to note two features of our writing style: our occasional use of contractions (for example, "we've" instead of "we have") and our avoidance of sexist language.

First, we have tried to make this book as down-to-earth and practical as possible. We imagine ourselves talking to you as we talk to our own students—trying to be direct, friendly, and helpful. Our prose is therefore rather informal and includes contractions. Academic papers, on the other hand, have a different purpose and are usually more formal. Some instructors might object to your using contractions in a formal sociology paper.

Second, we have deliberately used inclusive language when we refer to people in general. Historically, masculine nouns and pronouns have been used to refer to women and men both—for example, "*Man* is a social animal." As a result of the women's movement, this usage has become unacceptable. Chapter 5 explains ways of avoiding sexist language.

Finally, we wish we could show you some of the drafts of this book. Writing anything worthwhile—a paper or a book—is always a messy, frustrating, creative, and rewarding process. Our own experience has been typical. Final written work usually looks so neat that it's easy to forget the wastepaper baskets overflowing with outlines scribbled on scratch paper, penciled drafts, cut and pasted revisions, and annotated computer printouts. For example, the word-processing program on one of our computers automatically counts the number of times a finger touches a key as each document is typed. Writing Chapter 7 involved over 80,000 keystrokes, as we typed in material, rearranged it, changed it, added to it, replaced it, or erased it. So don't be discouraged if you don't like what you first write. That's normal. The paper will improve, and you will like it better with each succeeding keystroke or pencil mark. *A Guide to Writing Sociology Papers* will show you how this happens as it guides you through the writing process.

PART ONE
ESSENTIALS

Perhaps the most disabling myth about intellectual activity is that writing is an art that is prompted by inspiration. Some writing can be classified as an art, no doubt, but the art of writing is a trade in the same sense that plumbing or automotive repair are trades. Just as plumbers and mechanics would rarely accomplish anything if they waited for inspiration to impel them to action, so writers would rarely write if they relied on inspiration.

RODNEY STARK
Sociology

Writing is a craft as well as an art. As with any other craft, becoming a good writer requires understanding the principles of how papers work. A first-rate plumber must know some principles of hydraulics, and an outstanding auto mechanic, the principles of combustion. Writing a good sociological paper requires understanding principles of both sociology and writing.

Part I presents these fundamentals of craftsmanship. Chapter 1, "Getting Started," explains some topics that might be considered as much inspiration as perspiration, such as how to use a "sociological imagination" in writing. More specifically, this chapter covers some of the qualities that instructors look for in papers but that students sometimes have difficulty grasping. An instructor will frequently criticize student papers as being "not sufficiently sociological," "not addressing a real question," or "having problems of logic and structure." But often students are not sure what the instructor means, and instructors often find themselves at a loss how exactly to interpret their own comments. So we have explained what sociologists mean when they require papers to "take a sociological perspective," to "be logical and well structured," and to "answer a well-formed question."

Starting a paper at all and then staying on a productive schedule is troublesome for many students. Chapter 2, "Organizing Your Time," has some practical advice for these problems, both for papers assigned outside of class and for exams written in class. Chapter 3, "The Writing Process," recommends techniques for harnessing the power of the writing process itself to trigger insights and to continually clarify your ideas. Chapter 4, "Acknowledging Sources," explains when and how to introduce and cite borrowed information, and Chapter 5, "Polishing Your Paper," shows how to edit and format a final draft of your paper.

1

GETTING STARTED

Additionally, and especially in the social sciences, much unclear writing is based on unclear or incomplete thought. It is possible with safety to be technically obscure about something you haven't thought out. It is impossible to be wholly clear on something you do not understand.

JOHN KENNETH GALBRAITH
"Writing, Typing, and Economics"

Writing a good sociology paper starts with asking a good sociological question. Picking a topic is just the beginning of planning your paper. You need to frame your paper's topic in the form of a *question*. Asking a good question will make the other tasks of writing your paper much easier and will help you hand in a good finished product.

Everything else follows from the question your paper asks. Think of taking a photograph. The deepest artistic sensitivity or the most sophisticated technical skills cannot create a beautiful picture unless you point the camera in the right direction. But carefully aiming the camera in the right direction can combine with simple competence and a personal point of view to produce a fine and, if you are lucky, breathtaking photograph. Likewise, when you create a sociology paper, you can produce interesting, high-quality results without being the smartest or most eloquent student in the world: the key is to take the time to "point" your work in an effective direction by asking a well-formulated question.

Sometimes instructors assign papers by requiring students to respond to a particular question. When that happens make sure you thoroughly understand the question and keep it in mind as you work on the paper. Not answering the instructor's question is one of the most frequent pitfalls of student writing. Even if you have a thoroughly researched, insightfully reasoned, and eloquently written paper, if it does not answer the assigned question, most instructors will find it unsatisfactory. Read the

3

question carefully when you begin your work, reread it as you are doing any reading or research that may be required, reread it when you sit down to write, and reread it as you begin your final draft. People's minds, especially intelligent people's minds, have a tendency to drift to interesting and related, but not always pertinent, topics.

Even when the assignment is not presented as a question, you must formulate one to address in your paper. Three features distinguish a question that will serve as a strong foundation for a sociology paper. First, a helpful question reflects an understanding of sociology's distinctive perspective on human life. Second, it is carefully posed and framed. Third, it is asked in such a way that it lends itself to a logical and well-structured answer (in contrast to a question that suggests an endless list, such as "What are all the roles adopted by leaders?" or one that is too open-ended, such as "Why are people irrational?"). The following sections will help you to meet these three criteria for asking good questions.

WHAT IS SOCIOLOGY?

Failing to understand what sociology is and what sociologists do is a main reason that students experience difficulty in writing successful sociology papers. Since asking a good sociological question depends on understanding what sociology is, this section defines sociology and discusses how it is different from other fields.

Sociology is the study of human social behavior. Sociologists investigate how individuals are shaped by their social groups, from families to nations, and how groups are created and maintained by the individuals who compose them. Sociology's basic insight is that who a person is, what she or he thinks and does, is affected by the groups of which that person is a member. To begin thinking sociologically, look around and consider how the world may be experienced differently depending on whether a person is male or female, rich or poor, of one race/ethnicity or another.

Another part of sociology's insight is that interaction takes place in ways which are patterned, even though the people involved may be separated by many years or many miles or may appear to have differences. For example, societies at different historical times or in different geographical locations all find ways to enforce rules, to teach children valued beliefs, and to organize the production of goods necessary to their members' welfare. Sociologists try to understand the consistencies in these processes—the ways in which their similarities and differences follow a predictable pattern.

Finally, sociologists attempt to explain *in*consistency as well. How do new social patterns emerge? For instance, what accounts for changes in dating patterns, parent-child relations, or types of college degrees earned?

Sociology and Other Perspectives on Human Behavior

Sometimes new students (and more experienced ones!) are confused about how sociology is distinguished from other disciplines that study people, such as psychology, political science, history, philosophy, anthropology, and economics. In fact, these fields are not totally distinct. Right now, however, we want to focus on what is distinctive about sociology because, in order to write successfully in any discipline, you need to have some idea of its boundaries. Our brief sketch necessarily simplifies the definitions of sociology and its "neighbors" and exaggerates their dissimilarities. The differences we discuss here are intended primarily to sensitize you to sociology's distinctive features; they are not rigidly observed by theorists or researchers. In fact, many scholars describe themselves explicitly in terms that cross these boundaries (such as social historians, political economists, and social psychologists), often incorporating a sociological perspective into other disciplines.

The following summary compares and contrasts sociology with psychology, political science, history, philosophy, anthropology, and economics. We have illustrated their differences by showing how researchers in each field might approach one aspect of human life—deviant behavior.

Sociology and Psychology

Similarities: Both are concerned with attitudes, beliefs, behavior, emotions, and interpersonal relationships.

Differences: Psychology is more likely to focus on the individual level of human behavior. When sociology considers the individual, it is within the context of social groups.

Studying deviance: Psychologists investigate the categories of mental disorders underlying deviant behavior. A sociologist might try to discover whether members of one socioeconomic class are more likely than members of another class to be labeled "mentally ill."

Sociology and Political Science

Similarities: Both are concerned with government.

Differences: Political scientists analyze different forms of government and their underlying philosophies and study the political process. A sociologist is more likely to examine the interrelationship between political structure and behavior and other aspects of society, such as the economy, religious institutions, and the attitudes of various social groups.

Studying deviance: A political scientist might analyze laws regulating deviance. A sociologist might examine how such laws change as the members of society adopt different ideological beliefs or how they serve the interests of some classes more than others.

Sociology and History

Similarities: Both look at human life over time.

Differences: Historians are more likely to focus on the influence of in-dividuals and on the causes of specific events. Sociologists concentrate on the causes and effects of changes in patterns of social life, among both famous and ordinary people.

Studying deviance: A historian might interpret the motivations and ac-tions of influential deviant individuals and attempt to explain their in-fluence. A sociologist is more likely to trace changes in society's ways of defining and controlling deviant behavior.

Sociology and Philosophy

Similarities: Both are interested in beliefs about the nature of life.

Differences: Philosophy is a system of abstract reasoning that follows spe-cific rules of logic. Sociology is empirical: it seeks to discover information about the real world by gathering data about what people actually do.

Studying deviance: Philosophers might ask "What is good?" and "What is evil?" or analyze the appropriate uses of the term "deviance." Sociolo-gists stick to what actually goes on in the social world, asking, for instance, "What do members of this particular society or subculture believe is 'right' and 'wrong'?"

Sociology and Anthropology

Similarities: Both are concerned with social life, including culture, be-liefs, decision making, relationships, and so on.

Differences: Anthropology is more likely to study societies other than our own, and to compare aspects of society cross-culturally.

Studying deviance: Anthropologists might travel to an isolated, nonin-dustrialized society to study how it defines and treats deviant behavior. Sociologists would study the same processes by focusing on complex, in-dustrial societies.

Sociology and Economics

Similarities: Both are concerned with how society produces and dis-tributes goods and services.

Differences: While an economist concentrates on the economy in its own right, sociologists are more likely to consider how the economy affects and is affected by other social processes.

Studying deviance: An economist might study the contributions and costs of deviance to the gross national product. A sociologist might study how the control of the economy by upper social classes provokes deviant behavior, such as burglary and theft, by those without access to a fair share of goods and services.

THE SOCIOLOGICAL IMAGINATION

One way to describe what is distinctive about a sociological point of view is the "sociological imagination," a phrase coined by C. Wright Mills (1959). Using the sociological imagination means recognizing the connection between individual, private experience and the wider society. Mills calls the personal level an individual's "biography"; he uses the term "history" to refer to patterns and relationships on the larger scale of society.

As a student, for example, you have followed your own life path to college. Being a college student is part of your personal life story. Your family has its own beliefs about what a college education means. You have your own academic and career goals. You have individual feelings and attitudes about the subjects covered in your classes and your own mixture of college and work schedules. All these things make up your personal, *biographical* experience of your life as a college student.

Applying sociological imagination to your college life expands your perspective. It is like a wide-angle lens that allows you to see yourself in a larger, more complex (and, in many ways, more interesting) picture. Using sociological imagination, you can begin to see where your experience as a college student fits into the social world in which you live, the *history* of which your biography is a part. Perhaps you are part of a trend among your peer group to major in computer science or communication studies. It could be that you are part of an ethnic group whose members are underrepresented in higher education. Perhaps your academic goals have been affected by social values (say, an increasing emphasis on the need for a college degree), or maybe your career choice, combined with many others', will affect the way society's workforce is balanced between producing goods and providing services.

To use sociological imagination, then, is to identify the intersection of biography and history, the ways in which people are affected by social forces and social groups are affected by their members. As Mills (1959) himself puts it:

> Every individual lives, from one generation to the next, in some society; . . . he [or she] lives out a biography, and . . . he lives it out with some historical sequence. By the fact of his living he contributes, however minutely, to the shaping of his society and its history; even as he is made by society and by its historical push and shove. (P. 6)

Mills's deceptively simple insight—that people both affect their own destiny *and* are swept by currents of history—challenges and eludes sociologists from first-year college students just beginning to study the field to seasoned scholars. The key to using sociological imagination is to not lose sight of either side of this relationship.

SOCIOLOGY'S FOCUS AND METHODS

One of the major differences between high school and college is that in high school, "learning" usually means learning facts. Those high school students who demonstrate that they have learned the most facts generally earn the highest grades. In college, however, there is greater emphasis on analytical reasoning and thinking. Students are expected to understand entire systems of knowledge. Moreover, college students often find that there is more than one correct way to approach a topic; that is, that there is more than one *perspective* on an issue. A perspective is a way of looking at a topic. For example, think about the various ways of looking at a house. If you view it from the front, you see a door and windows with a roof overhead. If you look at the house from the side, you might see no doors, only windows. If you take your perspective from above, you see neither doors nor windows, only the roof. Although all three perspectives involve the same house, your observations from each perspective result in very different descriptions of that house.

Intellectual perspectives can differ as well. Earlier we saw how a number of disciplines take different perspectives on deviance. They all look at the same behavior, but each discipline paints a different description and develops a different explanation of it. Even *within* sociology there are several perspectives. Beginning students may find this confusing. For example, by adopting a *conflict perspective*, we can look at society in light of the ever-present conflict that goes on within it; by contrast, taking on a *consensus perspective* points us toward examining society in terms of the enduring ties that produce stable patterns of relationships among people. Likewise, whereas *microsociological perspectives* consider social life in terms of everyday interaction among small groups of people, *macrosociological perspectives* see things from the point of view of long-term change and societies as a whole.

To some extent these perspectives disagree about what we might generally consider the "facts" of society—about whether it is stable or conflicted, about whether it is defined by what occurs on a large scale or in direct interpersonal relations. More often than not, however, different perspectives are simply asking different questions. It's like looking at the house from different perspectives. A microsociologist might examine the process of becoming deviant from the deviant's point of view, whereas the macrosociologist might ask how definitions of deviance have changed over time. A sociologist operating from a conflict perspective might examine how deviance is produced as a result of the opposing needs of different social groups, whereas a colleague with a consensus perspective might ask how deviance serves to reinforce the rules of society. All of these perspectives share the features of sociology discussed earlier. All ask different questions—but within a sociological framework.

Some students struggle with the cognitive ambiguity that can arise when different perspectives with very different implications are all considered acceptable. This is one of the great intellectual feats of a college education: to be able to juggle more than one perspective in one's mind at the same time. As a novice sociologist, your task is to understand these different perspectives and to learn how to support whichever approach *you* take with empirical evidence.

Sociology not only encompasses a range of perspectives, but also allows sociologists to apply these approaches to questions about an innumerable array of topics. Like other disciplines, sociology has several major subdisciplines—variations on a theme, as it were. Some focus on large-scale "macro" phenomena, such as political activities or economic relations. Some focus on "micro" activities that occur on a face-to-face basis, such as in families, small groups, and work settings or among friends. Likewise, sociology may examine events that are as momentary as the eye contact between strangers on a bus or as long-term as the industrialization of society. It may deal with social life in terms of its structure, attempting to uncover stable, underlying patterns, or it may look at the fleeting interactional processes through which individuals relate socially.

In sociology classes, then, you might study anything from the sociology of sports to the sociology of religion. You might learn about how those engaged in different occupations perceive their work lives, how a thief accomplishes her or his crime, or how children learn table manners. You might study birthrates, medical decision making, or the sex lives of teenagers in the 1930s versus the 1990s. And, for each of these subjects, sociologists may disagree about the kinds of questions to ask and the methods to use in order to answer them.

It should come as no surprise, then, that just as there is no one "right" way to think sociologically, there is no single "right" way to do sociological research. Sociology's methods vary considerably. Most sociology texts and many instructors describe sociology as a "science." By this they mean that sociologists systematically collect information about the social world and then methodically analyze this evidence or "data." The data may come from any of a number of sources—from controlled laboratory experiments, from written accounts of social life, or from observing, interviewing, or surveying people involved in the phenomenon being investigated. (Part II of this book presents tips on how you can use four types of data sources commonly found in undergraduate sociology papers.)

Many sociologists literally *do* use scientific method, in much the same way that a botanist or chemist would: they set out to support or reject a prediction, or "hypothesis," about the relationship among several elements of the social world. To do that, they collect quantifiable data—information that can be transformed into numbers and analyzed statistically. (One example of this method is the survey research described in Chapter 9.) Those who adopt this "positivist" approach to sociology believe that we can observe and quantify the relationship between selected social variables (such as age, race, or gender) and particular social experiences (such as deviant behavior). After collecting and analyzing data on prisoners, for instance, the researcher might generalize about whether a twenty-year-old or a forty-five-year-old is more likely to end up in prison. The generalizations produced by these kinds of methods often form the basis of decisions regarding public policy, social programs, and the like.

However, not all sociologists see sociology as a science in the literal sense. Some sociologists believe that the complexity and subtlety of human experience make understanding social relations a very different endeavor than, say, measuring the effects of gravity on a falling object, as a physicist would do. Instead of quantifying social forces, these "interpretive" or "constructivist" researchers concentrate on probing how aspects of everyday life are constructed—given meaning—through social interactions. In studying deviance, for example, they might ask how (if at all) an individual who breaks the law comes to see herself as a criminal. Or they might explore how social interactions produce different ideas about deviance in different subcultures. To accomplish their goals, these sociologists use qualitative methods, conducting research that is quite different from that done in the biological or physical sciences. Examples of these methods include the participant-observation method and open-ended interviewing (discussed in Chapter 8). Rather than trying to generalize, interpretive sociologists want to specify in as much detail as possible just *how* the social world is constructed. Despite their different approaches, however, all sociologists base their conclusions on a combination of insight and carefully collected and analyzed evidence.

Although some sociology departments specialize in one perspective, topic, or method, most departments include faculty members who represent a range of sociological concerns and styles. Course curricula, including writing assignments, reflect this variety, and students typically have the opportunity to become familiar with several ways of asking and answering sociological questions. When you are trying to understand what an assignment requires of you, it will help to keep in mind the focus of the course as a whole and the particular approach your instructor is presenting.

Sociology, then, is a diverse field. But across all sociological methods and topics, *a sociological perspective involves seeing individuals interacting as members of social groups.* As you prepare to formulate the question that will underlie your sociology paper, remember that *adopting the sociological perspective is always the first step* in writing a successful paper.

FRAMING A QUESTION

Writing a good sociology paper requires using your sociological imagination to frame an interesting question that then guides your research effort. Asking a sociologically imaginative question is one of the tasks students find most challenging and most difficult to pin down. There is no magic recipe, but here are some tips that might help. Your instructor may feel that some aspects of what we say are more important than others, so remember that these are just suggestions.

Remember the "history" part of the sociological imagination. Avoid overly individualistic or psychological questions, questions that concern only what happens inside a person's head. For example, asking whether criminals are motivated more by aggression than by greed is more interesting psychologically than sociologically. (We are in no way implying that psychological questions are inferior to sociological questions, but our purpose here is to emphasize the sociological aspects of human life.) A sociologically imaginative question might ask what aspects of social life—such as race, class, or gender—influence people to act out their aggression or greed in socially acceptable or unacceptable ways.

Remember the "biography" part of the sociological imagination. Avoid overly economic questions that drop people out of the picture. (Again, economic questions are often interesting and important, but we want to emphasize the sociological aspects.) For example, asking how much income is lost to crime each year is less sociologically imaginative than asking what types of crime typically victimize wealthy people as compared to poor people.

Ask a question concerning *differences* between individuals, groups, roles, relationships, societies, or time periods. Only rarely do sociologists make claims about all people or all societies. They are typically more interested in how and why people or societies differ from each other; that is, they more frequently ask questions about variation than about uniformity. For example, they would probably not ask whether people are by nature aggressive but rather why some people are more aggressive than others. Are highly aggressive people socialized differently, part of a different subculture, vulnerable to different social pressures, or aspiring to different goals than less aggressive people?

The remaining five suggestions apply to questions for any discipline, not just sociology.

Ask a question that requires more than a simple "yes" or "no" answer. A "yes-no" question is a dead end. The case is already closed and there is nothing to investigate or argue. For example, the question "Does socioeconomic status affect marital stability?" can be answered "yes," and there is no more to say. So, too, with this question: "Can children born with severe language/communication deficits caused by aphasia be socialized to participate in society on a par with nonaphasic persons?" One way to improve such questions is to put the phrase "To what extent . . ." in front of them; for example, "To what extent does socioeconomic status affect marital stability?" Another remedy is to rephrase the question; for example, "What are the most effective ways for primary schools to enhance the normal socialization of children born with severe language/communication deficits caused by aphasia?"

Ask a question that has more than one plausible answer. The paper's task is to demonstrate why your answer is more valid than other plausible answers. You must argue why your answer is more correct and convincing than alternative answers. The question "What are the four crucial elements in the process of diffusion and adoption according to Everett Rogers?" has only one correct answer that can be checked by consulting what Rogers claimed. Nothing is left to argue. One way to improve this question would inject an element of interpretation by applying Rogers's model to a specific organization; for example, "How well does MADD (Mothers Against Drunk Driving) fit the four-part process of diffusion and adoption identified by Everett Rogers?" So, too, belaboring the obvious wastes both your time and your reader's. For example, whether there is widespread public opinion against violent crime can only have one plausible answer. No one would seriously claim otherwise. Before starting the research, specify different plausible answers to your question. Can you imagine anyone seriously taking the other side? If not, you need to reformulate the question.

Unless your assignment specifies otherwise, ask a question that draws relationships between two or more concepts. (Some exceptions are a definition paper, a "feeling" or reaction paper, and a story or narrative paper.) Typically, assigned questions concern the relationship between concepts. Are two concepts (for example, deviance and socialization) empirically associated or not? That is, are deviants likely to be socialized differently from nondeviants? Are two concepts (for example, social prestige and deviance) negatively associated; that is, when one is high, is the other low? For example, are people with high prestige less likely to engage in crime than people with low prestige? Unless specifically instructed, avoid questions that address only one concept, such as "What is deviance?"

Make sure you have access to the information to answer your question. Although some paper assignments do not require any research outside assigned readings and lectures, many do require you to document your points with evidence. For these papers, you must consider, when you ask your question, whether you can realistically get the necessary documentation. For example, "Has deviance always existed?" is an interesting question with important consequences for sociological theory. But it would be difficult to document adequately whether prehistoric societies had deviance or not. On the other hand, students are sometimes surprised to discover what information does exist and can be tracked down with a little work, so it is best to check with your instructor if you are unsure.

Make sure your question is answerable in the space allowed. This may be the most elusive of our tips and the one students falter on most frequently. Part of the difficulty is that some instructors expect finer detail of documentation or a more fully developed argument than others. Another problem is that students often don't know how much information they will find until they have done their research. Here are two guidelines. First, ask middle-range questions that are neither grand, monumental, deep truth questions nor minutely exacting, picky detail questions. Second, check out your question with your instructor before you begin your research.

To sum up this section, then, we want to stress that a good paper should not just be *about* some topic (such as mental health, race, gender, or occupations). For example, rather than a paper about social mobility, you might frame and address the question "Is there more opportunity for upward mobility in America today than there was a hundred years ago?" Notice that this question concerns differences between two fairly specific time periods. And it has more than one plausible answer; reasonable people could disagree about whether there is now more opportunity for mobility or less. Framing an answerable but debatable question is a fundamental, and sometimes the most demanding, part of writing a paper.

TERMS AND STRATEGIES IN ESSAY ASSIGNMENTS

When students are given a paper or essay assignment, they naturally want to know what the instructor wants, but asking "What do you want us to do on this assignment?" usually annoys the instructor. From the instructor's point of view, the instructions already indicate what students are expected to do with the information. Knowing the course content is not enough to do well on a paper assignment; knowing *what to do* with this content and having a strategy for selecting and presenting this information are essential. The way to determine such an appropriate strategy is to scrutinize the wording of the assignment, to clarify for yourself what is expected, and then to use a suitable strategy to produce the paper.

Instructors deliberately design assignments to get you to work with—and think about—course concepts and data in various ways. For example, writing about deviance could involve defining it, illustrating it, analyzing it, comparing it to other behavior, evaluating its effects, summarizing someone's theories about it, and so on. Sometimes instructors will provide you with a well-framed, unambiguous question to start with. At the other extreme, you may be given a very vague assignment ("Discuss deviance") that will require you to create and frame your own question. In the middle of this range are the following common commands that cue you to appropriate questions that can be framed concerning the course information and that tell you what the instructor wants you to do with this information.

Note that sometimes an assignment calls for more than one question because the instructor deliberately combines these commands, thereby requiring you to work with the material in several ways, applying several different strategies. At other times, instructors provide several different versions of essentially the same question but repeat it in different words to help you understand what you are supposed to do. If your assignment seems to call for several questions, first determine if they are the same single question in different words or if they involve separate strategies.

Analyze: Break something down into its parts; for example, a theory into its components, a process into its stages, an event into its causes. Analysis involves characterizing the whole, identifying the parts, and showing how the parts relate to each other to make the whole. Corresponding question: "What is the relationship between anomie and frustration in the functionalist theory of deviance?"

Assess/Criticize/Evaluate: Determine the importance or value of something. Assessing requires you to develop clearly stated criteria of judgment and to comment on the elements that meet or fail to meet those criteria. Corresponding question: "How useful is labeling theory for explaining why people join gangs?"

Classify: Sort something into main categories and thereby pigeonhole its parts. Corresponding question: "If someone cheats on an examination to get a better grade, which of Merton's forms of deviance does the behavior belong to?"

Compare/Contrast: Identify the important similarities and differences between two elements in order to reveal something significant about them. Emphasize similarities if the command is to compare, and differences if it is to contrast. Corresponding question: "What are the similarities and differences in labeling theory and functionalist theories of deviance?"

Define/Identify: Give the special characteristics by which a concept, thing, or event can be recognized; that is, what it is and what it is not. Place it in its general class and then differentiate it from other members of that class. Corresponding questions: "What is anomie? What behaviors or attitudes indicate that a person or group is anomic?"

Describe: Present the characteristics by which an object, action, person, or concept can be recognized or an event or process can be visualized. Corresponding question: "What is Durkheim's theory of deviance?"

Discuss/Examine: Analyze and/or evaluate a particular topic. You must decide on your own question concerning the things to be discussed. Instructors usually expect you to go beyond summary. Corresponding question: "What can sociological theories tell us about why gangs exist and why individuals join them?"

Explain/Justify: Make clear the reasons for or the basic principles of something; make it intelligible. Explanation may involve relating the unfamiliar to the more familiar. Corresponding questions: "Why do people break rules that they believe in? What theories do you think give the best explanation of this kind of behavior? What evidence can you present to support this theory?"

Illustrate: Use a concrete example to explain or clarify the essential attributes of a problem or concept. Corresponding question: "Give a concrete example of 'innovative deviance.' How does this example show the defining features of the concept?"

Interpret: Explain what the author of a quotation means (not what you mean). Corresponding question: "What does Durkheim mean by stating that animals cannot commit suicide?"

List/Enumerate: Give essential points one by one in a logical order. Corresponding question: "What are the forms of deviance in Merton's theory of deviance?"

Outline/Trace/Review/State: Organize a description under main points and subordinate points, omitting minor details and stressing the classification of the elements of the problem or the main points in the development of an event or issue. Corresponding questions: "What have been the major debates over deviance in the past quarter century? How has the resolution of one debate led into the next? Highlight these debates with reference to leading theories and path-breaking studies."

Prove/Validate: Establish that something is true by citing factual evidence or giving clear, logical reasons for believing it is true. Corresponding question: "Make a case on behalf of or opposed to labeling theory. What are the strongest justification and best evidence you can present to support your point of view?"

DEVELOPING AN ARGUMENT: LOGIC AND STRUCTURE

In writing, logic refers to the relationship between the paper's assertions and its evidence. Structure concerns how the parts of the paper fit together. If sentences are the "trees" of the paper, then logic and structure are the "forest." According to one faculty survey, structure and logic are among the most important criteria instructors weigh in grading papers.

Logic demands that a good paper go beyond mere assertion ("This statement is true because I say it is"). The answer to your question, which is your thesis, must be supported by evidence and reasoning. One way to accomplish this is to assume that the reader is naive (a Martian, for example) or skeptical. Try to imagine actively what a naive reader might not understand about what you are saying and explain your points to her or him. Try to imagine the kinds of doubts a skeptic might hold and attempt to convince her or him, just like a debater would.

Structure demands that in a good paper each sentence should be well written and make sense; each sentence should also be logically connected to the sentences around it, each paragraph to the paragraphs around it, each section to the sections around it, and all of them to the overall theme of the paper. Whether you write sentence by sentence or begin with a general plan and work down to the level of the sentence, by the time you submit the paper, you should be able to conceptualize the structure of the whole paper in your head (and, if necessary, to explain that structure to the instructor). This means being able to say in one or two sentences what the paper's main thesis is and how you go about arguing that thesis. Imagine your roommate or a friend asking "What's the point of the paper?" and "Why should the reader believe you?" If you can't answer those questions, you still have work to do before turning in the final draft.

The next step after framing your question is constructing a logical defense of your thesis—why your answer is more correct than alternative answers. This defense requires pieces of evidence that support your thesis. The evidence must be logically connected to the thesis so that you can make the statement (either in your head or in the paper) "If the evidence is true, the thesis is true." Many student papers (and some professional papers) falter here, presenting interesting and important evidence in narrative form, or in a controlled study, or sometimes through reasoned reflection, but then drawing a conclusion that is less than warranted by the evidence presented. So be sure to put aside the actual paper and think through the first three items on the checklist presented in Part III: "What is my thesis? Does my thesis remain evident and central throughout the paper? Have I supported my thesis with adequate evidence?"

Finally, the structure of the paper should reflect the logical connection of the evidence to the thesis. It is the writer's job, not the reader's, to draw the connections between evidence and conclusions and to show how the paper logically proceeds. Thus the paper's introduction, transitions, and conclusions are essential, not just incidental parts of the paper. The *introduction* should state the question that is being answered and specify the plan for answering it. As the paper unfolds, provide guideposts for the reader telling where the paper has gone and where it is going. These *transitions* indicate how sentences, paragraphs, and sections logically fit together. Transitions can be accomplished by including transitional words and phrases, such as "On the other hand" and "Furthermore." (See Chapter 3 for a list of transitions.) Or they can be stated in sentences: "The last section discussed Durkheim's basic presuppositions; this section will show how those presuppositions influenced his theory of religion." A common writing error is the *non sequitur,* a Latin phrase for sentences or paragraphs that have no apparent connection. They often result from a connection that is in the writer's mind but that she or he fails to demonstrate to the reader. A *conclusion* should remind readers where they have been and why you think the thesis has been demonstrated. Try to summarize the paper without repeating specific sentences. This is also the appropriate place to reflect upon the larger implications of your thesis—to answer the question "So what?" But it is not appropriate to present new evidence in the conclusion.

Two Formats of Logic and Structure

We suggest here two formats of logic and structure that are common in sociology papers. There are, of course, other formats that may be appropriate for specific assignments. If the paper assignment does not specify an explicit format requirement, it is often helpful to talk over your format ideas with the instructor.

▶ **The Three-Part Essay Format.** This type of paper is most commonly structured in terms of a major thesis (that answers a question) and three supporting "points."

There is nothing magical about the number three; it is a convenient number of points for the length and scope of papers typically written for course assignments. Each of the three points should logically support the thesis. You should be able to say "If point A (or B, or C) is true, the thesis is true." More precisely, in terms of formal logic, you need to be able to maintain that "if point A (or B, or C) were *not* true, the thesis would probably not be true."

Take as an example the thesis "Over the last hundred years, educational opportunities in America have opened up the American social structure to more upward mobility."

Point A could be: Educational achievement is more closely connected to high-status jobs than it was a hundred years ago.

Point B could be: Education is more equally accessible to all members of the society than were earlier means of determining people's status.

Point C could be: The content of education relates more to job skills than it did a hundred years ago.

The paper itself is structured around an introduction, discussion of point A, discussion of point B, discussion of point C, and a conclusion. The introduction presents the question that is being answered, the general thesis, and usually a plan of the body of the paper. Each point is discussed in turn. Each section usually starts with a claim—a statement of its main point. Often the next sentence is an example of this claim, followed by an explanation of how the example illustrates the point. Then you can elaborate on this point, identify its implications, take issue with some aspects, or provide other types of evidence. Finally, you need to tie it back in with your general thesis and with the argument so far.

You will need at least one paragraph for each discussion section, because that's what a paragraph is—a logical section with one main point. You may need more than one paragraph to deal with each main point, especially if the point is complicated or if you are presenting elaborate evidence. If you do, allocate separate paragraphs to each subpoint or aspect. This often happens when you want to analyze a particularly revealing example and explain to what extent it does, but also does *not*, illustrate a point you want to make. In other words, the discussion gives evidence and reasoning for why the point is true; the discussion also explains the logical connection between that point and the general thesis.

The conclusion then summarizes the overall argument and often offers your personal thoughts about the issue you have discussed.

A modified version of the essay format is also appropriate for a paper based on ethnographic research. If that is the kind of paper you're preparing, follow the structure described in this section, replacing the thesis and supporting claims with three major themes, or three points about a single theme, gleaned from your data. See Chapter 8 for details on this modified application.

▶ **The Journal Format.**   This is the format often found in articles in major academic journals such as the *American Sociological Review* and the *American Journal of Sociology.* The journal format is not the same as "journalistic style." The term "journalistic style" is sometimes used to describe the easy and fluid style of writing in popular magazines such as *Time, Newsweek,* and *Life.* The journal format refers to a particular way that a paper or article can be organized. One would almost never use the journalistic style of writing in a paper organized according to the journal format. The journal format follows the procedural logic of the "hypothesis testing" mode of conducting research, in which you formally test a specific hypothesis through systematic research. The journal format, although usable for projects other than formal hypothesis testing, is best suited to projects that include some sort of systematic data collection and analysis. Its structure follows this order: introduction (including the literature review and the statement of hypothesis), methods, results, and discussion. (See Chapter 9 on the quantitative research paper for more detail.)

The introduction specifies the question that is being answered in your paper and your general thesis. In this section, a "review of the literature" summarizes what other people have written about the topic, explaining why it is an important issue to study and what their answers are. This section should also formally state your hypothesis (for example, "A greater proportion of men today hold higher-status jobs than their fathers did a hundred years ago") and justify why you expect it to be true.

The methods section reports your research procedure, detailing where you got the data, how the variables were measured, and what sort of analysis you conducted on the data. A reader should be able to replicate your study by following the "cookbook" of your methods section.

The results section reports in literal terms what the study shows. For instance, "30 percent of men a hundred years ago were in higher-status jobs than their fathers, while 29 percent of men today are in higher-status jobs than their fathers," which is virtually no change. (These numbers are made up for this book. They are not accurate.)

The discussion section draws the conclusions and reflects upon the result—for example: "The hypothesis must be rejected. The occupational structure has not opened up. The American promise of an equal chance for all is not yet fulfilled."

The essay and journal formats are illustrated by sample student papers in this book. The paper on quantitative research (Chapter 9) follows the journal format. The remaining two sample papers—one based on ethnographic field research (Chapter 8) and one demonstrating a textual analysis (Chapter 6)—are modified versions of the essay format. See the relevant chapters for details on organizing your paper.

THE PROPOSAL

A *proposal* (sometimes called a "statement of intent" or even, misleadingly, an "abstract") is a preview of your paper. Instructors assign a proposal to get you started on your paper by framing a question and making a commitment to answering it. Obviously, your proposal can't describe your intended paper in much detail because at this stage you often don't know much about the topic. However, you can frame your question and provide a context for it. As such, the proposal is a quick introduction, usually only one or two pages long, to what you want to do. On the basis of this information your instructor can advise you about possible leads to follow up or alert you to problems that may snowball as you prepare your paper.

Your proposal should feature your question; for example, "To what extent is homelessness in Los Angeles attributable to mental illness?" In addition, it may include any of the following, depending on what you already
know or hope to find out:

- **related questions** triggered by your main question, such as: "What
  counts as 'mental illness'?"; "Who counts as 'homeless'?"; "Which
  comes first: the illness or the homelessness?"; "What drives people
  onto the streets?"; "How do people survive in these conditions?";
  "Where do homeless people go for help?"; "Why do some people get
  off the street while others don't?"
- **a provisional answer** to your question; in other words, your thesis.
  An example of this might be: "Many older homeless people behave
  eccentrically, but increasingly children and families are being made
  homeless and they are not necessarily mentally ill, at least not before becoming homeless." This provisional answer may be just a
  hunch or an "educated guess" based on course materials. You will
  definitely refine it as you learn more about your topic, and in the
  process you may change it entirely.
- **a *brief* statement of the personal reasons this question interests
  you;** for example, you can't help noticing more and more homeless
  people, you find their presence disturbing and frightening, and you
  are alarmed that not enough is being done to help them.
- **an academic justification for studying this topic;** that is, why it
  interests other researchers; for example, the increasing problem of
  urban homelessness for policymakers, for providers of social services, for public health and recreation, for tourism, and for others in
  addition to the homeless people themselves.
- **a sense of direction:** what you need to find out first and where you
  will start looking for it; for example, statistics on how many homeless people live in Los Angeles. Depending on how detailed a proposal your instructor requires, you may need to specify the steps
  you will take to answer the question. Some instructors want only a
  sense of direction indicating, for example, that you will be reading
  popular magazines and academic journals. Others want a more detailed methodological blueprint with a step-by-step plan listing variables or ethnographical site. In any case, you need to demonstrate
  that what you plan to do will provide an adequate answer to your
  question. This sometimes will also require acknowledging limitations on your answer; for example, we really don't know exactly how
  many homeless people there are because they are so difficult to
  identify. Moreover, some types of mental illness, such as paranoid
  schizophrenia, are easier to detect than other equally debilitating
  forms, such as severe depression. What all this means is that you

need to do some preliminary reading and thinking before you write your proposal.

A SAMPLE STUDENT PROPOSAL

Here is a sample proposal that student Daryl Williams wrote for a class on "Organizations and Society." The instructions for the paper were simply to "Write on an organization that relates to a concept discussed in class, and on a topic that interests you." A two-page proposal was assigned at the end of the first week of the quarter. Because Daryl did not yet know much about the organization he had selected, his proposal is understandably rather vague. Other proposal assignments could require considerably more detail.

OUR COMMENTS

Daryl begins by accounting for his interest in his chosen organization.

Daryl's instructor liked the informal tone and word choice of his proposal; for example, the word "indulge." Another instructor might have preferred more formality.

Daryl's question is a good start, but it needs to be refined. His instructor pointed out two initial problems here. First, the concept of an organization's motivation is very slippery, elusive, and hard to establish. What evidence establishes motivation: constitutions, public pronouncements, leaders, members, or actions of the organization? Organizations usually have a complex assortment of motivations, if they can be said to have motivations at all. Daryl's instructor suggested instead that he might study a particular instance, such as the AMA's position on various health insurance schemes, and modify his question accordingly.

Second, Daryl's question assumes that all professional associations attempt to control and regulate entire industries. This generalization is itself debatable. Another possibility, if it appealed to Daryl, would be to use the example of the AMA to *test*—not just *illustrate*—this assumption.

Here Daryl justifies the importance of studying this organization.

Daryl Williams
Sociology 168
7/16/90

PROPOSAL

Choosing an organization that interests me is hard because there are so many possibilities. Last quarter, though, I took a class on the sociology of medicine. This was a completely new and fascinating area of sociology to me, and my interest in it has been piqued ever since. In that class, we learned a little about the American Medical Association (AMA) which I found intriguing. Now, as the focus of my term paper on organizations, I have the perfect opportunity to further explore this group (as well as indulge in a bit more medical sociology).

I think that what I find most interesting about the AMA is that it is not necessarily the do-good organization that most people think it is. There is a popular misconception that the medical profession is in some ways more virtuous than other organizations. This is not true. Rather, the AMA, like other large and powerful organizations, has its own goals and interests, and acts primarily to defend or perpetuate them. In fact, I've learned that the AMA was specifically developed to keep a tight-fisted reign over the medical profession in such a way as to monopolize the medical industry. Hence, using the AMA as a case study from which I can generalize to include other organizations, my research question will be this: In what ways does the American Medical Association (AMA) exemplify an organization's attempt to control and regulate an entire industry?

I think this is a particularly important question to examine because it seems that large and powerful organizations everywhere are increasingly coming to dominate their respective industries. In other words, what the AMA is doing is not unique; rather, it represents an existing and growing trend. In addition, the AMA is a particularly useful model because it shows that all types of organizations—even the ones that we thought were more exceptional, professional, or noble than the rest—can behave in this manner.

Here Daryl identifies related questions triggered by his main question.

Daryl does not provide even a provisional answer to his question. He should have made some attempt at articulating a hunch.

Here Daryl identifies a sense of direction, but he should have offered more information about his sources of data. At the least he could have copied from his textbook some possible titles that he intended to consult in the library.

The content and tone of my research question raises several other questions: Why does the AMA wish to obtain such professional hegemony? At whose expense is this done? How is the AMA organized? What resistance does the AMA face? How is the AMA similar to other organizations? How is it different? I think these questions, and this research topic in general, merit study and attention. While my intentions are not to "expose" the AMA in any way, I think it is vitally important to assess the motives and actions of large organizations such as the AMA, because these groups play such a large and important part of both our social and personal lives.

I plan to begin by reviewing my notes from last quarter. My textbook for that class has some references about books and articles on the AMA that I can check in the library.

2

ORGANIZING YOUR TIME

It's worth repeating: half the battle is won when the first word is written. You wouldn't believe the wild contortions professional writers go through to avoid writing that first word of the day. Pencils must be sharpened; typewriters cleaned and ribbons changed; filing demands to be done; the cat must be let out; that filthy window must be cleaned; shelves of books must be rearranged; a letter must be mailed; the cat must be let back in.

GENE OLSON
Sweet Agony: A Writing Manual of Sorts

Good sociology *papers* argue a position that answers a question. So do good examination *essays*. But, unlike *papers*, exam *essays* obviously cannot go through a process of multiple drafts because they are written under pressure in class. Instructors usually assign *papers* to give you an opportunity to explore a topic and learn about that topic by writing about it. But they assign exam *essays* to see you demonstrate how much you already know. Because the purposes and circumstances of these two kinds of writing are different, each requires a different set of strategies for managing your time and resources.

WRITING PAPERS: THE TIME GRID

We believe that the key to writing better papers, with less anxiety, is starting early enough to write more than one draft. Many students experience "writer's block" because they think they should be able to produce a finished product on the first try. Paper writing, therefore, seems nearly impossible and is put off until the night before the due date. Then, because writing done at the last minute is often inadequate, the students' doubts about themselves as writers are confirmed. Some students move in a vicious cycle of anxiety, procrastination, and, almost inevitably, disappointing results. Making a time grid (see Figure 2-1) can help you to break this pattern and to feel more in control of the writing process by breaking up what may seem an enormous task into smaller "doable" tasks.

How do you eat an elephant? In little bites. A time grid is basically a specialized calendar on which you mark dates for these tasks, or "bites," taking into consideration your exams, other assignments, and other commitments. You can buy a ready-made blank student calendar in your campus bookstore, or you can hand-draw a blank time grid and photocopy it for reuse every semester or quarter.

The first task for all types of papers is choosing a topic, unless, of course, a topic is assigned. Select a provisional topic as early as possible, because it will probably evolve as you find references and become more familiar with the readings or the field setting. You can never know if a possible topic for a library or a quantitative paper will work out until you at least skim some possible sources. Nor can you finalize a topic for an ethnographic field research paper until you get permission to visit the setting and observe the people there.

Except for topic selection, different types of papers involve different tasks and therefore different ways of planning a work schedule. As you can see in Table 2-1, each type of paper requires a different set of tasks to be completed in a certain order. Study this table carefully because the way you allocate your time on your time grid depends on the type of paper you are writing. For illustration we have used the four most typical kinds of papers assigned in sociology classes: textual analysis, library research, ethnographic field research, and quantitative research. These kinds of papers are discussed in Part II.

To work with a time grid, begin by writing in the exams, quizzes, and major assignments from all your classes in the boxes corresponding to their due dates. Include any other important deadlines or events that may influence your writing schedule, whether school-related or not. Next, count backwards to determine a realistic date to begin each required task for your type of paper and write it in the corresponding box. So as not to clutter up the grid, make the beginning dates of new tasks also represent completion deadlines for the previous task. No matter what type of paper you are writing or how much time you have from assignment to due date, be sure to mark off enough time on your time grid to write and/or revise more than one draft. It is also advisable to build your schedule so that it ends *before* the absolute deadline, since unexpected events may keep you from meeting the due date.

The time grid will work only if you stick to it. Put it in a prominent place (for example, taped to a mirror or refrigerator) so you will see it every day.

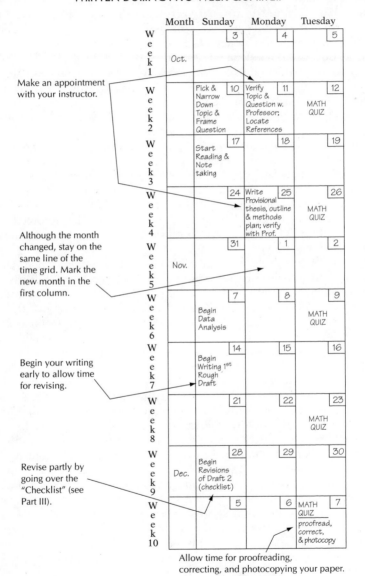

FIGURE 2-1
SAMPLE TIME GRID FOR A QUANTITATIVE RESEARCH PAPER
WRITTEN DURING A 10-WEEK QUARTER*

	Month	Sunday	Monday	Tuesday
Week 1	Oct.	3	4	5
Week 2		Pick & Narrow Down Topic & Frame Question `10`	Verify Topic & Question w. Professor; Locate References `11`	MATH QUIZ `12`
Week 3		Start Reading & Note taking `17`	`18`	`19`
Week 4		`24`	Write Provisional thesis, outline & methods plan; verify with Prof. `25`	MATH QUIZ `26`
Week 5	Nov.	`31`	`1`	`2`
Week 6		Begin Data Analysis `7`	`8`	MATH QUIZ `9`
Week 7		Begin Writing 1st Rough Draft `14`	`15`	`16`
Week 8		`21`	`22`	MATH QUIZ `23`
Week 9	Dec.	Begin Revisions of Draft 2 (checklist) `28`	`29`	`30`
Week 10		`5`	`6`	MATH QUIZ / proofread, correct, & photocopy `7`

Make an appointment with your instructor.

Although the month changed, stay on the same line of the time grid. Mark the new month in the first column.

Begin your writing early to allow time for revising.

Revise partly by going over the "Checklist" (see Part III).

Allow time for proofreading, correcting, and photocopying your paper.

* We have used the quantitative paper for our sample time grid because it has the most steps. Your time grid may have fewer boxes filled in than the one above.

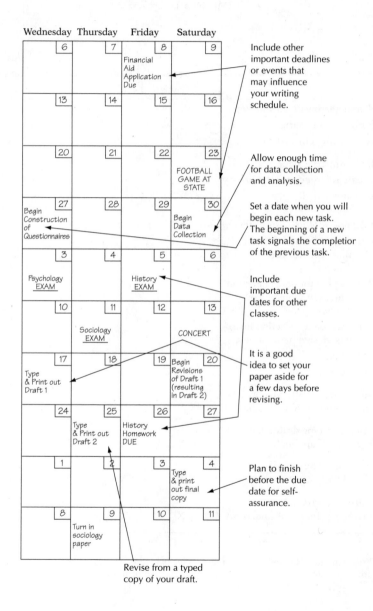

Wednesday	Thursday	Friday	Saturday
6	7	8 Financial Aid Application Due	9
13	14	15	16
20	21	22	23 FOOTBALL GAME AT STATE
27 Begin Construction of Questionnaires	28	29	30 Begin Data Collection
3 Psychology EXAM	4	5 History EXAM	6
10	11 Sociology EXAM	12	13 CONCERT
17 Type & Print out Draft 1	18	19	20 Begin Revisions of Draft 1 (resulting in Draft 2)
24	25 Type & Print out Draft 2	26 History Homework DUE	27
1	2	3	4 Type & print out final copy
8	9 Turn in sociology paper	10	11

Include other important deadlines or events that may influence your writing schedule.

Allow enough time for data collection and analysis.

Set a date when you will begin each new task. The beginning of a new task signals the completion of the previous task.

Include important due dates for other classes.

It is a good idea to set your paper aside for a few days before revising.

Plan to finish before the due date for self-assurance.

Revise from a typed copy of your draft.

TABLE 2-1
DETERMINING YOUR TASKS

	Textual Analysis	Library Research	Ethno-graphic Field Research	Quanti-tative Research
Pick and narrow down your topic; frame an appropriate question; verify with your instructor	X	X	X	X
Different middle steps:				
Locate references in the library		X	—[a]	X
Take notes on library references		X	—[a]	X
Take notes for analysis of text(s)	X			
Write a provisional thesis and outline; consult your instructor	X	X		X
Write a plan for data collection and analysis; consult your instructor			X	X
Construct data collection instruments, design methods, etc.				X
Collect data			X	X
Analyze data			X	X
Write a rough draft; type draft 1 (and print out, if applicable)	X	X	X	X
Revise; then type draft 2 (and print out, if applicable)	X	X	X	X
Revise, partly by going over the "Checklist" (see Part III)	X	X	X	X
Proofread, correct, and photocopy/printout of final draft	X	X	X	X

[a] These steps are not required of all ethnographic field research papers. You should check with your instructor to determine whether your assignment requires these two steps.

Many students find that the time grid not only helps them produce better papers but also keeps them on top of their other assignments. Our advice on organizing your time applies to short-term papers as well. Even when you have only a few weeks to complete your paper assignment, planning will pay off.

ORGANIZING YOUR TIME FOR ESSAY EXAMINATIONS

Essay exams test your thinking, not your ability to memorize details. What instructors want to see in your exam essay is the big picture—meaningful generalizations. They want you to demonstrate what all the details covered in class add up to. Therefore, the time you invest *before* you arrive for the exam is crucial. When you review, make the effort to pull the course content together into its main ideas.

BEFORE THE EXAM

Begin by reviewing the syllabus. Often it will identify course goals and main topics. Then study your lecture notes, particularly for the first and last lectures, because they often preview and summarize the course themes. Skim the assigned readings in your textbooks, paying special attention to headings and end-of-chapter study questions. Reduce your in-class organizing time by anticipating possible exam questions, preparing generalizations that answer them, and outlining support for these answers. (It is not necessary to write out a complete essay.)

Finally, take care of yourself. Get a good night's sleep, eat healthy meals, wear comfortable clothes, and avoid panic-stricken friends. Bring several pens to the exam.

IN CLASS

▶ **Examine the Exam.** Once you are in the examination room, spend at least five minutes reading through the exam sheet(s) *twice* in order to make choices, if they are available, and to ration your time. Otherwise, especially if you are nervous, you may confuse the number of questions or not understand important directions.

If you have a choice of questions, consider their relative difficulty. Which will you do your best on: one that is straightforward and safe, or one that is more challenging and will give you a chance to show off what you know? Once you make a choice, stick to it.

Determine how much time you have to answer each question, depending on its points. Setting such a time limit is especially necessary for good students who are tempted to go on and on to show how much they know. Remember that each question gets only a certain number of points. If you have more to say, leave a space at the end of your answer and come back later if possible.

► **Organize Your Answer.** Start with the question you feel most confident about answering, even if it's not in the first section of the exam. (Be sure to *label clearly* the number of each question as you answer it.) Other ideas will come to you as you write, and your relatively easy answer will build your confidence in tackling the others.

Underline or circle key words, such as "analyze," "evaluate," "how (in what way)," "how much (to what extent)," and so on. If the instructions simply say "discuss," you're on your own. Are there several theorists, institutions, concepts, or examples? Try a *comparison*. Does the question require demonstrated understanding of key terms? Try *defining* and *illustrating*. Is a process important? Try *analyzing* its different stages. Would grouping help? Try *classification*. For more information, see the list of terms in Chapter 1 (pp. 13–15).

One common essay exam strategy is to begin by cannibalizing the words in the question, using them as a ready-made part of your thesis answer. Here is an example:

> *Question:* In what ways has the subsequent development of the West confirmed or disconfirmed Marx's theory about class conflict in capitalism?
> *Answer:* The subsequent development of the West has disconfirmed Marx's theory about class conflict in capitalism in at least three ways. First, the class structure did not polarize into two unbridgeable classes, but instead gave rise to a very large middle class. Second, life chances for wealth and prestige now depend at least as much on education and occupation as on class background. Third, the revolutions Marx predicted in advanced capitalist countries did not occur, but instead Marxist-inspired revolutions have developed primarily in peasant-based societies.

Such a bald statement might be too obvious for a polished *paper,* but for an exam *essay* such an announcement can help you outline your answer and then stick to it.

Take a few minutes to plan what you are going to say before you start writing the essay, and ignore other students who may be rushing right into their answers. Make rough notes on the inside covers or back of your blue book, labeling them as "notes" for the reader. Brainstorm ideas. Jot them down and then group them into a provisional outline with the following parts:

Introductory paragraph. State your thesis and preview how you will support it. If you feel inspired, suggest why the subject is important. Here is where you usually define terms, if necessary.

Body. This is supporting evidence for your thesis, meaningfully collected under main ideas, taken one by one. You might be able to organize your evidence according to the pattern used to present the information in lectures. Otherwise, one of these common patterns may be suitable:

- *categories;* for example, race, ethnicity, region, or gender arranged in increasing or decreasing order of importance.
- *historical periods;* for example, preindustrial, industrial, postindustrial.
- *reasons;* for example, steps in an argument or links in a causal chain.
- *information* responding to specific subsections of the question posed.

Conclusion. You don't have to actually put the content of your conclusion in your outline, but you should preview what the conclusion will be. For example, your outline might read:

Conclusion

1. Summarize
2. What aspects of the answer not included here
3. So what? Why is this important?

▶ **Write Your Essay.** Identify the number of the question, but don't waste time copying out the question. Make paragraphs to block out main ideas from your outline. Use underlined or capitalized subheadings, as appropriate, to "announce" your main ideas. Plug in revealing details (facts, names, statistics, examples), and explain how these details work to illustrate the points you're making. Let the instructor know what you know.

Write *legibly* in ink. Print if you have to. The examiner must be able to read what you've written.

Skip a page between answers, or begin a new blue book for each essay. The empty space will be useful later if you want to add something. Cross out neatly; add neatly (if necessary, with arrows identifying the addition); and don't waste time with liquid correction fluid.

Keep track of the time you are spending. If you find yourself rushed, then cut back on details, summarize points, and put names, terms, and facts in parentheses instead of complete sentences. If you really can't finish, refer the reader to your outline and to your rough notes.

▶ **Finishing Up.** Always budget time for proofreading. Make sure your name and (if appropriate) the numbers of the questions are on the blue book(s).

Plan to see the instructor after the exam has been graded in order to review it. This practice has both pedagogical and practical advantages: you may learn something more, and, if you were disappointed by your grade, you might be able to clarify that a clerical error may have been made.

3

THE WRITING PROCESS

I told students that it didn't make much difference what they wrote in a first draft because they could always change it. Since what they put on a piece of paper was not necessarily final, they needn't worry so much about what they wrote. The only version that mattered was the last one.

HOWARD S. BECKER
Writing for Social Scientists

THE PERSONAL VULNERABILITY OF WRITING

Although we usually think of writing as an intellectual activity, a lot of personal feelings are at stake, especially when writing in college. When you write for a class, the writing is evaluated and most students feel that *they* are being evaluated, that somebody they barely know and have not had the opportunity to develop personal trust with is telling them whether they are worthy to be in college. That can be very scary. It's not surprising that students want to avoid such a risky activity. It is not made any easier by the common style of grading that tells students more about what is wrong with their work than what is good about it. For an excellent personal account of struggling with these feelings see "Risk" by Pamela Richards in Howard Becker's *Writing for Social Scientists*.

We can offer no easy solutions to the anxiety of writing or being evaluated. Few individuals, even professional writers, are ever entirely free of it. It may help to talk to your fellow students, teaching assistant, or instructor about your concerns. You will probably find that they (even the instructor) share the same feelings. The counseling centers at many colleges and universities have writing workshops designed to help alleviate your anxieties. In extreme cases, where "writer's block" prevents you from completing assignments or hurts the quality of your work, professional counseling may be appropriate.

Here are a few insights we can offer.

Different people have very different ways of composing a first draft. Some need to sharpen two pencils and make a cup of coffee; some can only write in the morning, others late at night; some can only type and others compose only in longhand. One of the authors of this book writes best while shoeless! None of these things matter, as long as the writing gets done. Students sometimes feel that there is a correct way to go about sitting down to write and that any personal quirks should be "cured." But they forget that writing can be an emotionally risky venture and that people often need little rituals to ease the tension. Just like the basketball player who caresses the basketball before shooting a foul shot, the baseball player who always knocks the mud off his shoes before stepping into the batter's box, or the ballerina who sits in the middle of the stage for five minutes before the curtain goes up, anything (provided it's legal and nondestructive) necessary to get ready for writing is appropriate as long as you don't do it *instead* of writing.

The secret to writing is rewriting. No one ever sits down and writes an excellent paper at one go. Believing that myth is a major cause of writer's block and anxiety about writing. Writing is definitely *not* a delivery system of ready-made ideas; it is a process of approximation. A writer works first by getting something down on paper—doodles, an outline, a provisional question or list of questions, a draft, or whatever—and then looks at it, likes some aspects and considers a way to develop those, dislikes some other aspects and thinks about ways to change them, and in so doing gets more ideas to jot down, and so the process continues.

The expression of ideas on paper necessarily goes through stages. But there is no One Right Way or One Right Direction to move through these stages. For example, some people like to begin by writing down everything that occurs to them in association with the general topic; they may even turn off their computer monitor and simply keyboard in everything they can think of. They then print this out, search through it for threads of thought and rich possibilities, and then outline some sequence of the previously jumbled, buried ideas. Other writers work out a highly structured outline first because the logical subdivisions help them spot and understand potential relationships between ideas. They then compose a draft, possibly beginning to write sentences and paragraphs about ideas somewhere in the middle or at the end of their outline. This is the way that student Alvin Hasegawa works (see his paper in Chapter 9). He recommends outlining before the first rough draft: "The only advice I can give to another student is to start writing the paper with an outline. An outline guides the direction of the paper, lets you get down something concrete to work with, and gives you an idea of what you have to do." However, we've said that the very act of writing triggers thought, so you may find that outlining comes more easily after you've written some ideas or after your first rough draft.

We therefore are not recommending any one particular way to move through this writing and rewriting process. However, we would like to share with you some suggestions about stages in it—particularly the value of outlining and revising, and about the nature of writing style.

A computer tip. Embed a symbol system as you keyboard your paper that you can use later to locate passages easily with the search command. This means use something like XXX to identify a place or places that you will want to find later, for example, to illustrate a point, explain an illustration, or complete a thought. Always refer to labels and figures by writing out the number ("Table One"). In that way you can use the universal "Search For" and "Replace" functions later to renumber them if necessary.

OUTLINING

Writing an outline can provide at least two benefits at different stages in the writing process: it can give birth to ideas and it can describe the connections between ideas that are already articulated. The first kind of outline is glorified doodling; the second kind of outline is a blueprint or a road map that tracks the relationship and sequence of main ideas in your paper. The first kind, to use C. Wright Mills's distinction in *The Sociological Imagination,* is private; its purpose is discovery, not presentation to others. The second kind can very usefully be shown to an instructor long before the paper's due date, to make sure you're on target. It is much easier to revise this second kind of outline (by adding, omitting, or shifting main parts) than it is to repair a completed paper.

DISCOVERY OUTLINES (PRIVATE, JUST FOR YOUR EYES)

1. **Freewriting.** This is brainstorming or free association. Just write nonstop for 5–15 minutes with no censoring of your ideas. If you are keyboarding on a computer, dim the screen so you're not distracted, and at the end of 15 minutes scroll back to find some key words or phrases you like, underline them, and then immediately use the "Insert" command to add 5–10 more minutes' worth of thoughts.

2. **Lists.** Make up a shopping list of all the ideas or questions that you can think of that you associate with or might need in any way for your paper, just as if you were going to the store for groceries. Then group them

into families. This is easy to do on a computer with the "Move" and "Indent" commands.

3. **Reporter's Notebook.** Consider the famous journalism questions "Who?" "When?" "Why?" "Where?" "What?" and "How?" and try to create information related to the general topic for each question.

4. **Diagrams.** Some people are visually oriented and like to see their ideas emerging as pictures on the page. Here are several different kinds of diagrams you can try:

- *Clustering.* Write one key word or phrase (for example, a person's name, an issue, a term) in the middle of a sheet of paper. Circle it and then write down related concepts and examples in their own circles elsewhere on the page. Draw lines between the circles to indicate various logical relationships between all these items.
- *Branching.* Build a tree from a key word or phrase. Analyze it into its branch ideas and then into the twig and leaf ideas. Your tree can be vertical, horizontal, or upside down.
- *Columns.* Set up a compare-and-contrast table in two columns. Include in each column the information that fits under the things you are juxtaposing.

A computer tip. Computer programs exist for outlining ideas, such as MORE II and ACTA for the Macintosh. Some word-processing programs, such as Microsoft Word, have outlining capabilities. Your own word processor may have such an outlining function. If so, learn how to use it. If not, use the "Indent" command to create, copy, and save an outline. You may want to use it later to begin drafting your paper by inserting material. Open two files so you can access and move information between two corresponding windows: (1) your notes and/or outline and (2) your developing draft of the paper. Most writers move back and forth between their outline and rough draft as work on one modifies the other.

Presentation Outlines (public, to show to others)

This is a completed set of ideas, arranged in a specific sequence. As such it's a map or blueprint of the paper itself. It can be a topic outline composed of words and phrases like a table of contents, or it can be a sentence outline. In either case, a proper presentation outline signals the order and relationship of ideas through visual layout (headings and indentations) and through a symbol system, either an alternating number-letter system (roman numeral, capital letter, arabic numeral, lowercase letter) or a number system (1, 1.1, 1.1.2, and so on).

REVISING

Once you have written a more or less complete draft of your paper, your next step is to revise it. Revising can greatly improve the logic and structure of your argument (these two features of your paper are discussed at length in Chapter 1). You need the "big picture" of a complete draft on which to work. Therefore resist the temptation to revise individual bits of your paper as you write your draft, or you may spend too much time fiddling with a small part instead of getting a complete draft done.

Revising includes inserting new ideas and deleting or modifying old ones; rewriting sentences or paragraphs to improve clarity or logic; moving sentences or paragraphs around to strengthen organization; and adding transitions to enhance the flow of your writing and accentuate the relationships among your ideas. Setting your draft aside for a few days between revisions helps you see its strengths and weaknesses more easily.

Most writers rely on three revision techniques: *eliminating wordiness, adding details and examples,* and *adding transitional expressions.* Following is a sample paragraph from a student's draft proposal for a paper on stress management. Note that the paragraph is grammatically correct but is not well written. Then you will see how the student applied each of the three revision techniques to improve the paragraph.

Original draft paragraph:

> From the readings I did for the course on stress, I have found that there have been many studies done to try to find the single most common cause of stress. Some stress scholars believe it is the major life changes that provoke stress. Others believe that it is the everyday hassles and annoyances of life which bring about stress. Despite the conflicting viewpoints in the causality of stress, all scholars agree that when stressful stimuli can be recognized and regulated early there seem to be less damaging effects on the body. At this point I have a confident feeling that I will be able to locate good, current information on the questions of stress management, which I intend to research. (121 words)

1. **Eliminate Wordiness** The following can lead to wordiness in writing:

- Redundant pairs ("everyday hassles and annoyances")
- Inflated phrases ("At this point")

- Intensifiers ("single most common")
- Action in a noun rather than a verb ("a confident feeling")
- Passive voice ("be recognized and regulated")
- Expletives ("it is")

Paragraph revised to eliminate wordiness:

According to my readings about stress, many studies have tried to find its most common cause. According to some scholars, major life changes provoke stress; for others, every-day annoyances cause it. Despite conflicting explanations, all agree that early recognition and regulation lessen bodily damage. I feel confident now that I can locate good, relevant information on stress management. (58 words)

2. **Add Details and Examples**   Details answer the journalistic questions *"Who?" "When?" "Why?" "Where?" "What?"* and *"How?"* Examples can be illustrations that you create or evidence that you cite.

Paragraph revised to add details and examples:

According to my readings about stress, many studies have tried to find its most common cause. *Adolescent Stress: Causes and Consequences* (1993) includes 14 chapters by different social scientists. According to some scholars, major life changes provoke stress; others argue that everyday annoyances cause it. Two paradigms predominate: the "stress model," especially in medical sociology and psychology, and the "normative development" model, especially in child development research. Despite conflicting explanations, all agree that early recognition and regulation lessen bodily damage. I feel confident now that I can locate good, relevant information on stress management. (94 words)

3. **Add Transitional Expressions**   Transitional words function like traffic signals, directing the reader from one sentence to the next by identifying the logical relationship between these sentences.

- *To show addition:* again, also, and, and then, besides, equally important, further, furthermore, moreover, next, similarly, too, what's more
- *To show time:* after, afterward, as, at length, at once, at the same time, by, earlier, eventually, finally, first, formerly, gradually, immediately, later, next, once, previously, second, soon, then, thereafter, while

- *To make the reader stop and compare:* after all, although, at the same time, but, conversely, for all that, however, in contrast, in the meantime, meanwhile, nevertheless, nonetheless, notwithstanding, on the contrary, on the other hand, still, whereas, yet
- *To give examples:* as an illustration, for example, for instance, in other words, to illustrate, to demonstrate
- *To emphasize:* as a matter of fact, clearly, in any case, in any event, in fact, indeed, more important(ly), obviously, of course, that is
- *To repeat:* as I have said (demonstrated, argued, noted, etc.), in brief, in other words, in short
- *To draw a conclusion:* accordingly, as a result, at last, consequently, hence, in brief, in conclusion, in sum, on the whole, so, therefore, thus, to conclude

Paragraph revised to add transitional expressions:

According to my readings about stress, many studies have tried to find its most common cause. For example, *Adolescent Stress: Causes and Consequences* (1993) includes 14 chapters by different social scientists. According to some scholars, major life changes provoke stress; however, others argue that everyday annoyances cause it. Two paradigms predominate: first, the "stress model," especially in medical sociology and psychology, and, second, the "normative development" model, especially in child development research. Despite conflicting explanations, all agree that early recognition and regulation lessen bodily damage. I therefore feel confident now that I can locate good, relevant information on stress management. (100 words)

Note that this final, revised paragraph still includes fewer words than the original draft. However, every word adds meaning. The result is clear, concise, logical writing.

When revising, think carefully about your paper's key concepts and terms. Define them as you introduce them (usually in the opening paragraphs) and use them accurately throughout the paper. Be especially cautious when using terms originated by sociologists that have become part of everyday language and yet retain special sociological meanings (for example, "stereotype," "status," "self-fulfilling prophecy"). If you are unsure, we recommend that you consult one of the following specialized dictionaries in the reference section of your college library: *A New Dictionary of the Social Sciences, A Modern Dictionary of Sociology,* or *Dictionary of Modern Sociology.* It's often helpful to write out sociological definitions of your central terms on scratch paper—in language you can understand—in order to foster clear and accurate use of them as you revise. When dealing with words that do not have special sociological meanings, a good dictionary and a thesaurus can help you both to locate the most precise word that expresses what you want to say and to find synonyms for varying your word choice.

A computer tip. Desk accessories are now available that include such references as the *American Heritage Dictionary of the English Language* and *Roget's Thesaurus. Writer's Toolkit,* for example, includes these as well as other references, such as collections of quotations. Check to see if your campus computer lab provides such resources to use at this revising stage.

The revising stage is also the time to troubleshoot your draft for sexist language. Have you inadvertently used sexist language (such as used the masculine pronoun "he" exclusively)? Although most writers prefer to use nonsexist language, repeating "he or she" (or "she or he") every time a singular pronoun is required can sound awkward and repetitive. An occasional "he or she" sounds fine; but two in one sentence or, say, three in one paragraph are distracting. Sometimes writers solve this problem but create another by following a singular noun or pronoun with the non-gender-specific, but plural, pronouns "they" and "their." For example, here is a paragraph from Alvin Hasegawa's paper in Chapter 9:

> As far as ethics are concerned, this research was pretty fair. Our surveys were anonymous, so no one would feel as if they were giving up intimate secrets for everyone to see. The only ethical issue that might arise would be if a subject discovered that he or she was in a low-prestige ranking or if he or she found out that he or she did not date. Of course, the subject knows whether he or she dates, but the survey may rub it in. The realization that one does not date may result in lowering self-esteem.

In what looks like an admirable attempt to write in a nonsexist manner, Alvin erroneously changes a singular pronoun to a plural one ("so no one would feel as if they . . .") and then uses four *he or she*'s in close proximity. In many cases you can easily manipulate language so that it is both nonsexist and grammatically correct by using plural subjects, which can be followed, quite correctly, with "they" or "their." Here is one possible revision of Alvin's paragraph:

> Ethically, this research was pretty fair. Our surveys were anonymous, so respondents would not feel as if they were giving up intimate secrets for everyone to see. The only ethical issue that might arise would be some subjects' discovering that they were in a low-prestige ranking, or if they found out that they did not date. Of

course, the subjects know whether they date or not, but the survey may rub it in, resulting in lowered self-esteem for some respondents.

Finally, it's a good idea to locate a manual of style—which presents standards and examples of grammar, punctuation, usage, and typography—to answer specific questions that may arise during the writing process. If your paper includes tables and graphs, choose a manual that also provides guidelines on how such information should be arranged and labeled. (The style manuals we recommend below include such guidelines and are available in many libraries and bookstores.) Early in the quarter/semester, before the almost inevitable end-of-the-term crunch, ask your instructor to recommend a manual; you can put it aside until you need it. If your instructor doesn't have a preference, you may choose the inexpensive paperback *ASA Style Guide,* now available from the American Sociological Association (1722 N Street NW, Washington, DC 20036-2981), which is very useful, but brief (38 pages), or *The Chicago Manual of Style* (long and comprehensive, but currently available only in hardcover at what may be a prohibitively expensive price). We also recommend the inexpensive, popular paperback edition of Kate L. Turabian's *A Manual for Writers of Term Papers, Dissertations, and Theses,* which recommends many of the same style standards suggested by *The Chicago Manual of Style.* If anxiety about standards and rules impedes your writing, don't even think about a manual until you have generated at least one draft.

A NOTE ABOUT STYLE

Some people try to compensate for uncertainty with verbal bravado: using big words and complex sentence structures to sound intelligent. Sociologists have been frequently criticized for using too much jargon and writing in a convoluted style that is difficult to comprehend. Some students try to copy that style, thinking that it will make their writing seem "academic." That defeats the purpose of writing, which is to communicate. The best writing is usually easy to read and understand. The intelligence is in the ideas, not the vocabulary. Students too often think that if they sound intelligent they will get a better grade than if they write intelligently. Occasionally an instructor will give a higher grade to papers with fancy words, but most look more closely at the ideas.

So remember these tips:

- Don't use a big word where a small one will do.
- Use contractions (for example, "it's," "don't," "you're") as you draft your paper if they feel more natural to you than writing the words

out ("it is," "do not," "you are"). Before you revise your final draft, however, ask if your instructor objects. If you have waited until the last minute and do not know your instructor's preference—which may vary according to the type of assignment—then play it safe and avoid contractions (for example, they are not appropriate for the journal format).

- Use specialized sociological terms only to be precise about the concept you are discussing.
- Each sentence should include only one thought or idea.
- Try to use active rather than passive verbs wherever possible to ensure that both writer and reader know *who* is "doing the doing." Too much use of the passive voice can create ambiguity about the social processes under discussion.
- Try to avoid using too many prepositional phrases, which can fill sentences with modifiers of modifiers and make them difficult to read.
- Use adverbs and adjectives carefully. Some people think that good writing means filling your text with flowery adverbs and adjectives. Make sure that the modifiers you use add meaning and not just filler to your text.
- Remember that reading your paper should be a pleasure, not a chore.

4

ACKNOWLEDGING SOURCES

Pray be precise as to details.

SHERLOCK HOLMES IN CONAN DOYLE'S
"Adventure of the Speckled Band"

Research is a collective effort. Scholars build on and respond to each other's data (concepts, insights, theories, statistics), which circulate from one scholar to another through conference papers, articles, and books. Academic conventions have developed to keep track of whose ideas are being borrowed, used, and reused, so that accuracy can be checked and credit for this valuable information can be given to the proper authors. You, too, as an apprentice scholar are engaging in this research process when you write a paper; and you, too, are expected to follow these conventions for identifying what you borrow from others. By acknowledging your sources in proper citations and references you avoid plagiarism.

AVOIDING PLAGIARISM: WHEN AND WHAT TO CITE

Plagiarism is an academic offense. It is theft of intellectual property, of someone else's ideas and words. It is cheating that presents another writer's words or ideas as if they were your own. Plagiarism is taken very seriously in colleges and universities and can be grounds for expulsion. Professional scholars are similarly bound to avoid plagiarism, by such guidelines as those in the American Sociological Association's *Code of Ethics*.

Instructors can usually detect intentional plagiarism. Their years of study have made them familiar with the articles, books, and textbooks in their fields. When a student copies this writing into a paper, instructors recognize the sound and shape of the prose. Even if they can't immediately tell what page it comes from, they know it is not the student's original work. Also, plagiarized papers usually do not resemble the student's authentic writing style, which the instructor has read before, for instance, on midterm examinations.

You can avoid unintentional plagiarism by making careful notes that respect the integrity of the sources you use, and by identifying exactly where you got these borrowed words or ideas that you later use in your paper. The rule goes this way: you don't need to cite common knowledge, but you must acknowledge any author's private intellectual property—any presentation of information that is uniquely the author's. *You must cite such borrowing whether you quote it directly or paraphrase it.*

When you cite borrowed information, beware of two problems: (1) borrowing too much of the original language without quoting it, which is plagiarism, and (2) distorting the source and thereby paraphrasing it inaccurately. Following are examples of these two kinds of problematic citations from a source.

The original source:

It has been argued that anorexia nervosa has characteristics similar to culture-bound syndromes. A culture-bound syndrome may be defined as a constellation of symptoms which is not to be found universally in human populations but is restricted to a particular culture or group of cultures.

Nasser, Mervat. 1988. "Culture and Weight Consciousness." *Journal of Psychosomatic Research* 32(6):573–77.

1. Too much of the original source:

Anorexia nervosa has many characteristics of a culture-bound syndrome. Nasser (1988), the writer of "Culture and Weight Consciousness," says, "A culture-bound syndrome may be defined as a constellation of symptoms which is not to be found universally in human populations but is restricted to a particular culture or group of cultures" (p. 573).

In the first sentence of this paragraph, too many words from the source are used without quotation marks even though the second sentence is a quotation. This is therefore an example of plagiarism.

2. An inaccurate distortion of the original source:

Using a theory about culture-bound syndromes, Nasser (1988) claims that anorexia nervosa tends to spread from person to person within a culture, but rarely goes outside of that culture (p. 573).

This statement misrepresents the source's position.

Here is a good way to cite borrowed information from this source:

As Nasser (1988) notes, some people feel that anorexia nervosa may be usefully compared to the phenomenon he describes as a "culture-bound syndrome" (p. 573).

Do not worry that your paper will be unoriginal if you include many citations. Precise and full citation is one of the features that instructors look for when assigning quality grades; it shows that you have done some real work. *If you are in doubt, always cite your sources.* Err on the side of overdoing it.

Students often have difficulty determining whether an idea is common knowledge (which doesn't need to be cited) or an author's unique insight (which needs to be cited). The term "anomie," for instance, was coined by Durkheim. Does that mean that if you write the word "anomie" in a paper about the contemporary urban underclass, you are borrowing Durkheim's idea and word and must therefore cite him? No, not necessarily. You might want to mention Durkheim to invoke his authority, but the term doesn't belong exclusively to Durkheim any more. Over the years "anomie" has become part of every sociologist's working vocabulary; the concept is common knowledge and therefore doesn't need to be cited. However, let's say that you read a book or article about the urban underclass in which the author makes an important point using the concept of anomie. If you borrow that author's point for your own paper, then you must cite him or her (but not Durkheim) as your source. Remember, too, that you must cite your sources when you borrow anything unique to those authors: their words when you quote exactly, and their ideas when you paraphrase.

IDENTIFYING YOUR BORROWED WORDS OR IDEAS

Every time you weave a borrowed idea into your paper you have two alternatives, depending on how you recorded this information on a note card. First, you can quote or paraphrase the borrowing. Second, you can rely on a parenthetical citation alone to identify the source of the borrowing, or you can name the source in the text of your paper.

Quoting a source directly means extracting a word, phrase, sentence, or passage, and inserting it into your own paper. Quoted information should be enclosed within double quotation marks or, if lengthy, indented as a block quote. Quote only when the original words are especially powerful, clear, memorable, or authoritative. Otherwise, paraphrase.

There are two minor changes you may make in a quotation, neither of which changes its meaning. These two legitimate changes are illustrated in our own quotation from C. Wright Mills's *The Sociological Imagination* (1959):

> Every individual lives, from one generation to the next, in some society; . . . he [or she] lives out a biography, and . . . he lives it out with some historical sequence. By the fact of his living he contributes, however minutely, to the shaping of his society and its histor; even as he is made by society and by its historical push and shove. (P. 6)

First, notice that we omit some of Mills's sentence, again without changing the meaning, and we indicate this omission by a punctuation mark called "ellipses," three spaced dots. If the ellipsis points came at the end of the sentence, they would be preceded by a period—hence, four dots. Second, we are uneasy about Mills's use of "he" to refer to all humankind and want to make the language inclusive, so we add our own words "[or she]," inserting them within square brackets into Mills's quotation.

Another possible addition within square brackets is the Latin word *sic*, meaning "so," which you can use when you want to quote original words that contain an error.

Paraphrasing means condensing the author's meaning and translating a passage into your own words. This is a perfectly acceptable practice and, in fact, an important skill to develop. Paraphrasing forces you to think through and actively understand what you have read. But if you use another's idea when writing, you must give that person credit with a citation, even if you are presenting the idea in your own words.

There are good and bad ways to paraphrase. Here is an original passage from Emile Durkheim's *Suicide* (1951) followed by examples of good and bad paraphrasing:

> The term "suicide" is applied to all cases of death resulting directly or indirectly from a positive or negative act of the victim himself, which he knows will produce this result. . . . This definition excludes from our study everything related to the suicide of animals. Our

knowledge of animal intelligence does not really allow us to attribute to them an understanding anticipatory of their death nor, especially, of the means to accomplish it. . . . If some dogs refuse to take food on losing their masters, it is because the sadness into which they are thrown has automatically caused lack of hunger; death has resulted, but without having been foreseen. . . . So the special characteristics of suicide as defined by us are lacking. (Pp. 44–45)

Following are two examples of bad paraphrasing. In the first, the writer has shifted words around in the sentences and replaced individual words by plugging in synonyms. The writer has not genuinely condensed or translated the author's meaning into her or his own words; this problem is usually compounded by a failure to cite the source (in this case, Durkheim):

When some pets stop eating because their owners have left, this is caused by the unhappiness into which they have fallen, which necessarily makes them lose their appetite: the final end that ensues, however, was not anticipated. Therefore, the unique features of suicide as described by our definition are missing.

In the second example, the writer has changed the order but kept the words the same. Again the writer has not condensed the passage or translated it into her or his own words; and, again, this problem is usually compounded by a failure to cite the source:

Lost masters cause their sad dogs, refusing food, to lack hunger. The dogs die, not foreseeing this result. What is lacking is our special characterization of suicide as we define it.

A good paraphrase boils down the original idea and puts it in your own words. Here is a good paraphrase:

EXAMPLE: According to Durkheim (1951, pp. 44–45), animals, such as abandoned dogs who starve themselves, do not commit suicide because they do not understand the connection between death and the means of causing death.

Remember that even good paraphrasing requires citing the source of the borrowed *idea* being presented.

CITATIONS IN THE TEXT

Let's say that you are writing a paper on some aspect of suicide and that you want to use this insight from Durkheim. You have a choice of four legitimate ways of weaving it in. Study these four examples:

- Animals do not commit suicide (Durkheim 1951, pp. 44–45).
- Suicide necessarily involves knowledge of the consequences. "This definition excludes . . . everything related to the suicide of animals" (Durkheim 1951, p. 44).
- According to Durkheim (1951, pp. 44–45) animals do not commit suicide, because committing suicide involves understanding the consequences.
- Durkheim (1951) argues that suicide involves knowledge of the consequences. In his words, "This definition excludes . . . everything related to the suicide of animals" (p. 44).

Note that the first two examples rely entirely on the citation within parentheses to identify the borrowed idea. The last two examples put some of that parenthetical information in the text of the paper itself, in what is called "a running acknowledgment" (it "runs" in the paper, and it "acknowledges" the source).

When you *paraphrase*, all the information (name, date, and page number) goes inside one parenthesis at the end of the paraphrased idea, unless you name the author in a running acknowledgment, in which case the date and page number go inside one parenthesis immediately after you name the author.

When you *quote*, all the information (name, date, and page number) goes inside one parenthesis at the end of the quoted idea, unless you name the author in a running acknowledgment, in which case the date goes inside one parenthesis after the author's name, and the page number goes inside another parenthesis at the end of the quotation.

When you use a running acknowledgment, don't always rely on "states," as in "Durkheim states that. . . ." ("Feels" is even worse.) Instead, experiment with some of these verbs and other similar examples: "argues," "contends," "maintains," "claims," "reports," "charges," "concludes." You can also use various phrases for a running acknowledgment; for example, "according to Durkheim" or (for a quotation) "in Durkheim's words."

How do you choose among these four citation options? Consider the reader. How important is it for the reader to know immediately, in an emphatic way, where the idea comes from? Is it the idea itself (as in the first two examples above) or is it the source (as in the last two examples above) that is most important?

FORMAT

The following format guidelines from the American Sociological Association (ASA) describe how you should cite borrowed information in your paper, whether paraphrased or quoted. (Your instructor may want you to use some other standardized format, such as the published guidelines of the American Psychological Association [APA] or the Modern Language Association [MLA].)

In the ASA format, authors' names used in the text are followed by the publication date in parentheses. The page number follows the date; or in the case of a direct quote, follows the quotation.

EXAMPLE: Goffman (1981, p. 180) disputes the notion that mentally ill patients are hospitalized primarily for treatment. Instead, he believes that they are institutionalized so that they can be controlled.

EXAMPLE: Goffman (1981) claims that the goal of hospitalization "is not to cure the patient but to contain him in a niche in free society where he can be tolerated" (p. 180).

If you don't name the author in the text of your paper, enclose the last name, year, and if appropriate, page number(s), within parentheses at the end of the borrowed thought:

EXAMPLE: The treatment of the mentally ill in this country can give the impression that the goal of hospitalization "is not to cure the patient but to contain him in a niche in free society where he can be tolerated" (Goffman 1981, p. 180).

When you write a textual analysis (see Chapter 6), you might use only one source—the book or essay that you are analyzing. In this case, you need to give the publication date only once—the first time the author's name is mentioned.

EXAMPLE (first mention of author in textual analysis): Durkheim (1951) claims that suicide is not only an individual event but also a social phenomenon.

EXAMPLE (after second mention of author in textual analysis): Durkheim describes the role of social factors in suicide.

Note that the page number of quotations, or of specific claims or evidence, should be indicated even after the first mention of the author.

EXAMPLE: Durkheim (p. 44) defines suicide in a way that leaves all animal deaths out of his study.

Full publication information on the text you use for your analysis should be included in your list of References (discussed later in this chapter).

At times you may want to cite several authors who discuss a single idea. Then you will have a series of citations that should all be enclosed within parentheses. The way you should order them depends on which style system you are using. Some systems prefer date order; others prefer alphabetical order. Still others list authors in order of their contributions.

EXAMPLE: Some sociologists question the value of using official statistics in conducting research (Kitsuse and Cicourel 1963; Cicourel 1964; Matza 1969).

For dual authorship, give both last names. For more than two authors, give all last names the first time you refer to the source; in subsequent citations to that source, use the first name followed by *"et al."* (But include all the authors' names in the References at the end of the paper.) For sources with six or more authors, use the first author followed by *"et al."* throughout.

EXAMPLE: Many sociologists believe it is important to examine the work of the professionals who claim to treat the physical and mental health of a society (Yarrow et al. 1955; Conrad and Schneider 1980).

For authors with more than one publication in the same year, designate each work by adding an "a," "b," and so on to the year of publication, in the order mentioned in your paper.

EXAMPLE: Norbert Elias's *What Is Sociology?*, listed below under "Examples of Listings for Books," would be cited in the text as (Elias 1978b).

If the quotation is longer than five lines, present it in block-quotation form. Indent all lines five spaces from the left margin (leave the right mar-

gin as it is throughout the text) and single-space. Quotation marks are un-
necessary, since the indented left margin tells your reader that the material is quoted. The quotation from Durkheim, discussed earlier in this
chapter under "Avoiding Plagiarism," is an example of a long quotation.

In rare cases, you may also use the block-quotation format when you
want to emphasize especially important or interesting quoted material.
For example, in Chapter 8, the writer of the sample student paper uses
the indented format to highlight a quotation that is particularly dramatic
but only three lines long.

NOTES

In some disciplines, sources are cited in footnotes (which appear at the
bottom of the paper's pages) or endnotes (which are grouped together at
the end of the paper). In sociology, however, source citations are incorporated into the text. Notes, if there are any, follow the references and
relay information that may be of interest to the reader but is not directly
relevant to the paper's thesis. Avoid using notes as a way out of organizing your paper by making them a "dump" for materials you are not sure
how to integrate. Add notes sparingly, only to express a tangential comment that you feel you *must* make.

REFERENCES AND BIBLIOGRAPHIES

The text of your paper is followed by a list of the source materials you used
in writing it. Some instructors prefer that you list all materials you consulted in developing your paper, whether or not they are directly incorporated into your paper; in this case the list is entitled "Bibliography." Others prefer you follow the format of most sociology journals, listing only
those materials actually cited in your paper; in this case, the list is entitled "References." Check with your instructor to see which type of listing
is preferred, but remember that in *both* cases you must list your sources
for all borrowed ideas, whether they are directly quoted or paraphrased.

Listing sources you found online (as we tell you how to do in Part II)
presents special problems, because electronic databases are often updated frequently, making it impossible to locate your exact source later
on. A few style guides have begun to include guidelines on electronic citations; but, if you are using electronic sources, it is best to consult your
instructor for his or her preferences regarding how they should be listed.

When you are compiling your Bibliography or Reference section, list
all sources alphabetically by the author's last name. Under each author's
name, list works according to the year of publication, beginning with the

earliest date. Do not separate the list into sections for "articles," "books," or other sources; a single list is sufficient. In the examples that follow, note the order of the information and how it is punctuated, underlined (or *italicized*, which is equivalent to underlining), and abbreviated. When formatting this section, place the heading at the left-hand margin, type it in all capital letters, and triple-space between the heading and the first source listed. The quantitative paper is an exception. In a quantitative paper, center the heading REFERENCES. (See the end of the sample quantitative paper, p. 185, for an example.)

When the source you have cited has more than one author, all authors' full names should be included, in the same order in which they appear on the book's title page or after the title of the article. Alphabetize under the first author's name. The first author should be listed last name first and the other author(s) should be listed first name first.

If no author is named for a source, then list the information in alphabetical order according to the organization responsible for publishing it.

Examples of Sources with No Named Authors

Los Angeles Times. 1992. "The Congressional Races." 25 Oct., p.T6.
SPSS, Inc. 1988. *SPSS-X User's Guide.* 3d ed. Chicago: SPSS, Inc.
U.S. Congressional Budget Office. 1988. *Trends in Family Income: 1970–1986.* Washington, DC: U.S. Government Printing Office.

Use the following examples of various kinds of source materials as models for capitalization, spacing, indentation, and punctuation. For additional models, check the format of citations and reference entries in any issue of *American Sociological Review.* Here are some general tips.

1. Is the work a *book* whose entire main text is written or edited by the same author or authors? If so, note that in this format titles of books are underlined (or italicized) in the References or Bibliography list. If a book was first published many years ago, include the original publication date in brackets before the more recent date. For more than one book published in the same year by the author(s), identify each work by adding "a," "b," and so on to the year of publication.

Examples of Listings for Books

Cheatham, Harold E. and James B. Stewart, eds. 1990. *Black Families: Interdisciplinary Perspectives.* New Brunswick, NJ: Transaction.
Durkheim, Emile. [1897] 1951. *Suicide.* Translated by J. A. Spaulding and G. Simpson. Glencoe, IL: Free Press.
Elias, Norbert. [1939] 1982. *The Civilizing Process. Vol. 2, Power and Civility.* Translated by E. Jephcott. New York: Pantheon.

———. 1978a. *The Civilizing Process. Vol. 1, A History of Manners.* Translated by E. Jephcott. New York: Urizen.
———. 1978b. *What Is Sociology?* Translated by S. Mennell and G. Morrissey. New York: Columbia University Press.
Emerson, Robert, ed. 1983. *Contemporary Field Research.* Boston and Toronto: Little, Brown.
Palmer, John L., Timothy Smeeding, and Barbara Boyle Torrey, eds. 1988. *The Vulnerable.* Washington, DC: Urban Institute Press.

2. Is the work an *article* published in a *journal?* Give the volume number of the issue in which the article appears, followed by a colon and page numbers to help your readers locate the article.

Examples of Listings for Journal Articles

Lichter, Daniel T., Felicia B. LeClere, and Diane K. McLaughlin. 1991. "Local Marriage Markets and the Marital Behavior of Black and White Women." *American Journal of Sociology* 96:843–67.
Parnas, Raymond I. 1967. "The Police Response to the Domestic Disturbance." *Wisconsin Law Review* 4:914–60.

3. Is the work found in an edited *collection of articles* or in an *anthology?* If you are referring to a specific article in the collection, the citation goes under the name of the author of the article and includes the name of the anthology and the editor(s) within the reference.

Examples of Listings for Collections

Goffman, Erving. [1969] 1981. "The Insanity of Place." Pp. 179–201 in *The Sociology of Mental Illness,* edited by O. Grusky and M. Pollner. New York: Holt, Rinehart and Winston.
Smolensky, Eugene, Sheldon Danziger, and Peter Gottschalk. 1988. "The Declining Significance of Age in the United States: Trends in the Well-Being of Children and the Elderly Since 1939." Pp. 29–54 in *The Vulnerable,* edited by J. L. Palmer, T. Smeeding, and B. B. Torrey. Washington, DC: Urban Institute Press.

4. Has the information been communicated during a *class lecture?*

Example of Listing for Lecture Notes

Lopez, David. 1992. Class lecture. 21 Oct.

5. Did any information in your paper come from *machine-readable data files (MRDF)?* If so, you must also identify the source of this kind of sur-

vey data. Note in the following examples that you must describe it as an
MRDF, and identify its producer and distributor, author, date, title, and
place of origin, as well as the organization responsible for it. The code-
book accompanying a data file often contains an example of a biblio-
graphical reference for it. Look for this example on the back of the code-
book's title page.

Examples of Listings for Machine-Readable Data Files (MRDFs)

American Institute of Public Opinion. 1976. *Gallup Public Opinion Poll #965*
 [MRDF]. Princeton: American Institute of Public Opinion [producer]. New
 Haven: Roper Public Opinion Research Center, Yale University [distributor].
Boothe, Alan, et al. 1992. *Marital Instability over the Life Course [United States]: A
 Three Wave Panel Study, 1980–1988* [MRDF]. Lincoln, NE: Department of So-
 ciology [producer]. Ann Arbor, MI: Inter-university Consortium for Political
 and Social Research, University of Michigan [distributor].

5

POLISHING YOUR PAPER

It has long been an axiom of mine that the little things are infinitely the most important.

SHERLOCK HOLMES IN CONAN DOYLE'S
"Adventure of the Copper Beeches"

First impressions count. What your paper *looks* like is important. Its appearance will create expectations in the instructor who picks it up to read and grade. A professional-looking paper promises quality. So take the necessary trouble at this last stage to proofread and polish your draft. Now the most difficult parts of the writing process are behind you. In fact, some writers who do anything "to avoid writing that first word" (see the quotation at the beginning of Chapter 2) actually *enjoy* polishing.

Think of polishing as a way of showing hospitality, and your reader as a special guest whom you would not dream of putting to work. In some cases, your paper will be among dozens that your probably overworked instructor or reader must evaluate. Imagine your own irritation if, after reading students' papers for hours, you picked up one that was printed with a faint ribbon that should have been replaced long ago; or, conversely, imagine your sigh of relief and gratitude when the next paper in the stack is easy to read. Although a nicely presented paper that lacks substance will not likely fool even the weariest instructor, studies reveal that a professional-looking paper implies a smart and serious student and often contributes to a better grade. Taking the time to "package" a carefully written paper also shows respect for your instructor's workload—a respect that he or she may well be inclined to return.

At this stage you are on the last lap, but do not underestimate the importance of a strong finish. Therefore, allow ample time for a careful—not rushed—polishing of your paper. Doing so can often turn "poor" into "satisfactory," "good" into "excellent."

EDITING

Edit your draft to find and correct inadvertent errors in spelling, punctuation, repeated words and phrases, and omitted words. After you print
out what you hope will be your last draft, get away from it—for several
days if possible, or for a good night's sleep at least. Efficiency in spotting
weaknesses increases dramatically with distance from the paper, and
flaws that escape your bleary eyes at 2 A.M. often leap off the page when
you are rested.

The way to spot such mechanical problems is to proofread. To proofread efficiently, you must *see,* not just *look at,* your draft. The way to *see*
errors is to examine a hard copy of your paper (not just a computer
screen) to engage hand, brain, and eye coordination. Take a pen or pencil and then point to each word as you read it silently, or, better, out loud,
to yourself. Only through this hand movement will you make yourself actually see what you have written; otherwise you will be consulting your
short-term memory and will literally not see your draft. Once you have
proofread your paper, have someone else proofread it, too.

A computer tip. Most word-processing programs have spellcheckers.
Use your spellchecker to detect and correct misspellings. There is no ex-
cuse for spelling mistakes in a word-processed paper. But do not depend
on your spellchecker alone to edit your paper.

Especially be on the alert for these two common problems in word-
processed papers that spellcheckers cannot detect: (1) repeated passages
in the paper that you moved from one location to another but did not
delete from the first location, and (2) incorrect sentence structure caused
through revising on the computer. As an example of this second problem,
consider this sentence in a revised draft: "This paper will to show how
Robert Parks' model of racial and ethnic group contact explains Latino
discontent about the recent UCLA student body elections." The author of
this mangled sentence originally wrote "The purpose of this paper is to
show how . . ." and then changed it to "This paper will show how." But
when she edited her draft she did not completely delete the original
phrase.

Two popular computer programs that go beyond spellchecking in order
to check grammar and style, too, are *RightWriter* and *Grammatik 5.* Although not foolproof, they can be useful aids. So, if you are editing your
paper in your campus computer lab, investigate whether a grammar and
style checker program is available for your use.

Corrections. Despite your best efforts, however, you may need to make
some last-minute corrections. Even though there should be no hand-
written corrections on a word-processed paper, it is better to correct any
mistakes by hand than pass in an uncorrected paper. Here are several of

the most common corrections, which can be made in ink by using conventional proofreader's marks.

To insert, put a caret ($_\wedge$) just below the line at the place where you want to insert and then write in the word or phrase directly above the caret.

EXAMPLE: This is what you do if you have left$_\wedge$a *out* word or phrase.

To delete, put a single line through the word or phrase.

EXAMPLE: the ~~good~~ word

If you neglected to indent a paragraph, put the paragraph sign (¶) right before it.

FORMATTING

Begin by setting up the following automatic features on your computer. Use the tabs, not the space bar, for measurement (for example, one inch, not eight spaces) so that the format remains constant when you print out your text, even if you change fonts, pitch, or typeface.

- Margins (one to one-and-a-half inches on all sides)
- Double-spacing (quotations longer than five lines should be single-spaced and indented one inch from the left margin)
- Paragraph indentions (one-half to one inch)
- Left margin justification. Do not justify the right margin; a ragged right margin is friendlier and the spacing between the letters often looks better.
- A header with your last name and the page number only

Word processing turns writers into designers. The creative possibilities of printing out a final draft, once the completed draft has been saved in the computer's memory, can be very satisfying. Here is an opportunity to experiment with typeface, pitch, font, italics, boldface, boxes, borders, underlining, etc. Unfortunately, the result is sometimes a mess and distracts the reader from your ideas. To avoid this problem, keep these design principles in mind:

- Make the shape follow sense. What you do to the printed words should emphasize their meaning. For example, Helvetica Narrow 12 point is excellent for tables and other types of writing that require lots of information in a very small space. Zapf Chancery is a display face that gives headings a decorative look. New Century Schoolbook looks traditionally academic.

- Use restraint. If you emphasize everything, nothing stands out.
- Use your page preview function or scroll through the document to identify and repair "widows," which are single lines separated from the rest of their paragraph by a page break, or other breaks such as captions separated from figures.
- Stick with 12-point fonts. Smaller ones are hard to read, especially on a dot-matrix printer. Since legibility is important, use a reasonably new ribbon or cartridge.
- Use your italics function to indicate titles of publications, which on typewriters need to be underlined.
- Use the bold command for emphasis, not italics, underlining, or capitalization.
- Simplicity is best. Just because you can create elaborate headers and footers, for instance, doesn't mean that the reader needs all that information.

If you use a title page, center your title horizontally and place it halfway down the page. In the lower right-hand corner, put your name, the course number (for example, Sociology 101), the name of your instructor, and the date. Number pages beginning with the first page of the text, not with the title page. Sometimes instructors do not require a title page for short papers (approximately five or fewer pages). If you're not using a title page, provide the same information (your name, the course number, the instructor's name, and the date) in the upper right-hand corner of page 1; triple-space and center the title; and triple-space again before you begin the first paragraph.

A quick review of Chapter 4 will remind you of the proper form for citing sources in the text of your paper and for the list of References that follows the text.

Depending on the type of paper you've written, some instructors may want you to include your raw data, statistical calculations, questionnaires, observation checklists, instructions to respondents, ethnographic field notes, or other items. As appropriate, you should make each of these items an appendix to your paper. (*The American Heritage Dictionary* defines "appendix" as "supplementary material.") The appendix belongs after the References or Bibliography on a separate, titled page. If your paper requires more than one appendix, number or letter each one (Appendix 1, Appendix 2; or Appendix A, Appendix B, and so on). Number the pages of the appendix(es) as if they were additional text pages—if, for example, the last page of the text is numbered 5, the first page of the appendix would be 6.

You may single-space or double-space an appendix depending on the nature of the material and how it can most easily be read. The spacing need not be the same for all appendixes. However, the heading is ordinarily centered and triple-spaced—that is, you triple-space between "Appendix" and the title and triple-space again between the title and the body of the appendix.

Many computer programs allow you to import figures from other files into your paper, but if you feel overwhelmed by the technology, you can manually cut and paste them into the appropriate place in your paper and photocopy the page.

As with any work created on a computer, save your document often and back it up on another diskette or a hard disk. For insurance against hardware problems, make an extra copy on a floppy disk.

PART TWO
WRITING FROM VARIOUS DATA SOURCES

As to Holmes, I observed that he sat frequently for half an hour on end,
with knitted brows and an abstracted air, but he swept the matter away
with a wave of his hand when I mentioned it. "Data! data! data!" he
cried impatiently. "I can't make bricks without clay."

DR. WATSON IN CONAN DOYLE'S
"Adventure of the Copper Beeches"

The goal of a sociology paper is to develop a thesis in response to a question about the social world and to support that thesis with evidence. But where does the evidence come from?

There is no one answer. As we indicated earlier, sociology is diverse. Data may be gathered from many sources and by several methods. The next four chapters present guidelines for writing papers based on four data sources: textual analysis (Chapter 6), library research (Chapter 7), ethnographic field research (Chapter 8), and quantitative research (Chapter 9). They reflect the most typical writing assignments in sociology classes, and they use or modify the formats described earlier: essay and journal (see Chapter 1). Three of the four chapters can be used from the first day of your first sociology class. Since quantitative research, however, depends on specialized ways of collecting and analyzing information, the last chapter will be more useful if you are taking or have taken a basic course in quantitative methods.

An annotated sample paper, written by an undergraduate sociology student, concludes each chapter in Part II, except the chapter on library research. The sample papers illustrate our guidelines. You can match them up with your own papers and use our marginal comments to check what you have written yourself.

Rather than include a sample library research paper in Chapter 7, we have instead presented information about specialized sociology reference sources because we have found that students are likely to be familiar with the library research paper from their previous English classes.

You will find the guidelines for using library references very valuable, particularly those on *Sociological Abstracts* and the *Social Science Citation Index*, keys to the vast sociological literature in the library. Although our list of reference sources is not exhaustive, it will get you started in the right direction.

Papers almost always require you to do some outside reading even when data are drawn primarily from another source. For example, quantitative papers entail reviewing the literature to determine similar empirical studies of the topic, which means evaluating the books and articles that report these studies. For this reason, Chapter 6 on textual analysis is relevant to library, ethnographic field, and quantitative research as well.

Before we turn to the chapters on these sources of data, however, we need to discuss some important skills for locating useful data and other information online.

LOCATING AND ASSESSING ONLINE INFORMATION

Two skills are becoming especially important as student writers increasingly rely on computers at home and in their college library to locate information electronically. The first skill is *conducting online searches* of academic databases (such as your library's catalogs or CD-ROMs) on the Internet (such as email discussion lists or the World Wide Web) in a way that is not overly time-consuming and that does not result in an overwhelming amount of undifferentiated data. The second skill is *judging the data* you locate online: sorting out the authoritative and useful data from the distracting and useless information that inevitably turns up online.

Online information is increasingly available on any sociological topic. Anyone with a computer, a modem, and a telephone line can find a wealth of Internet information without ever leaving home. Regardless of the kind of paper you are assigned or the types of data you are expected to use, then, some relevant online information is quite likely available to help you understand and write about your topic. For example, the student who wrote the sample textual analysis paper in Chapter 6, which discusses one of Norbert Elias's books, could have consulted the World Wide Web site Norbert Elias and Process Sociology at <http://www.arts.su.edu.au/Arts/departs/social/elias/elias.html>. Maintained by Professor Robert van Kriken at the University of Sydney in Australia, this site explains, among other things, how to join the Elias-I listserv and how to consult its archives. So, too, the student who prepared the ethnographic field study of the ways that mental illness is perceived and treated by the courts (see Chapter 8) might very usefully have consulted the MacArthur Research Network on Mental Health and the Law at <http://ness.sys.virginia.edu /macarthur>. This World Wide Web (WWW) collection, organized by researchers at the University of Virginia, provides an overview of the issues of adjudicative competence, treatment competence, coercion, and violence risk, among other features. Such an overview of basic concepts would be a helpful beginning point for the student about to undertake this ethnographic study. As a final example, the student who investigated the influence of prestige on student dating choices (see Chapter 9) could have used the Internet relay chat (IRC) function in the Web site Courtship Corner at <http://www.talkcity.com/courtship> to conduct informal, exploratory interviews online or to confirm initial findings.

There are two general ways to begin looking for online Internet data. First, you can use the search capacity of your Web browser, such as by activating the Net Search box on Netscape, or you can go directly to a search engine, such as AltaVista or Yahoo! Second, you can go to a specialized Web collection of linked sites, such as WWW Resources for Sociologists at <http://socsci.colorado.edu/SOC/links.html> maintained by Professor Susan Brumbaugh at the University of Colorado at Boulder. Once at this site, you can then follow links off it to specialized online resources, including sociology-related email lists, newsgroups, and online publications; social science data archives; activist and feminist resources; criminology, demography, and family sociology resources; and miscellaneous resources on student travel, jobs, and funding and grants.

The availability of vast amounts of online data is a relatively new phenomenon. Not only must you learn how to locate relevant online data, but you must also determine the value and usefulness of the information you find. Academic sources are usually dependable because they have been put together by professional librarians. However, unlike information channeled through library databases, much of the information on the Internet, and especially on the World Wide Web, is questionable. Some Internet sites are excellent sources of reliable information. But the information on other sites may be inaccurate and misleading because almost anybody can easily "publish" information on the World Wide Web without scrutiny by legitimate scholars. The information may look trustworthy even if it isn't. As we will show you, there are ways to protect yourself against deceptive Internet information. Before you can evaluate online information, however, you need to know how to discover it. Searching for online information efficiently requires special techniques that involve using Boolean operators, which are explained in the following section. For more help, consult a college librarian. In addition, your college library may provide handouts about or offer classes in online search techniques.

SEARCHING ONLINE INFORMATION WITH BOOLEAN OPERATORS

Boolean operators are logical relationships. Most undergraduates use only two Boolean operators when they search online sources: OR and AND. These Boolean operators allow you to use a computer to search for data sources tailored specifically to your topic.

Consider what you would have to do instead, if you relied on bound volumes of indexes and abstracts. Let's say that you want to investigate mental illness among the homeless in Los Angeles. If you used paper,* you would have to consult a number of different sections in different volumes, locate the volumes on various shelves, and look for separate information about mental illness, and then separate information about homelessness, and then separate information about Los Angeles.

With a computer, however, you could combine these concepts using Boolean operators and thereby search for them simultaneously. You would find, for example, that the University of California has over 10,000 books on the subject of Los Angeles, 2,283 books on mental illness, and 596 books on homelessness, but that it has only one book in its collection on all three subjects. If the computer is given the right commands, it could find information about this book in about three seconds: *A Study of Homelessness and Mental Illness in the Skid Row Area of Los Angeles* by Rodger K. Farr, published by the Los Angeles County Department of Mental Health in 1986.

To make the computer perform this online search, however, you must first tell it exactly what terms to look for, such as words in titles, authors' names, Library of Congress subject headings, or keywords. In our example, the computer found the book by looking for words in titles *(mental illness, homelessness, Los Angeles)*. Note also that you can enlarge or shrink the scope of the search by using the Boolean operator OR or AND. In our example, the computer combined title words with AND *(mental illness* AND *homelessness* AND *Los Angeles)*.

You are probably already familiar with using two general categories to find library information: (1) authors' names and (2) the subjects they

---

*We are *not* suggesting that paper is unimportant. Indeed, paper is often essential: many sources, such as *Women's Studies Abstracts* and *Alternative Press Index,* are indexed and abstracted only on paper. In addition, electronic databases often do not go back very far in time.

have written about. Online searching provides you with the opportunity to search with at least two more categories: (3) titles of sources, as in our example, and (4) keywords associated with sources.

SEARCHING WITH KEYWORDS

Technically, a *keyword* is a word that may be located in the title of the source, in the Library of Congress subject heading for the source, or even in the abstract of the source if the database provides abstracts. For example, an online search for articles, combining the keywords *mental illness, homelessness,* and *Los Angeles* with the Boolean operator AND, found this source: a journal article by Paul Koegel, M. Audrey Burnam, and Rodger K. Farr entitled "Subsistence Adaptation among Homeless Adults in the Inner City of Los Angeles" (see the following figure). Note that the keyword *mental illness* appears only in the article's abstract. A search by title words alone would not have found it. Not all databases use keywords. However, keywords are particularly useful, and we recommend that you start an online search with keywords if they are available.

SAMPLE OF ONLINE INFORMATION FROM A
LIBRARY CATALOG DATABASE

Search request: F KW HOMELESSNESS AND KW MENTAL ILLNESS AND KW LOS ANGELES
Search result: 1 citation in the Magazine & Journal Articles database

Display: 1 AB

1. Koegel, Paul; Burnam, M. Audrey; Farr, Rodger K.
    Subsistence adaptation among homeless adults in the inner city of Los Angeles.
    Journal of Social Issues v46, n4 (Winter, 1990):83 (25 pages).

Abstract:
    Author Abstract: This article describes the subsistence-related activities of homeless adults in Los Angeles' downtown area, and examines whether homeless people with chronic disorders such as major mental illness and/or substance abuse differ from those with no chronic disorder in their subsistence adaptation. Findings indicate that homeless people use multiple resources over short periods of time. While minor differences between those with and without disorders were apparent, the general lack of differences between these two groups was most striking, suggesting the leveling quality of homelessness. Differences between individuals with various chronic disorders indicated that those with chronic substance abuse, and particularly those with both substance abuse and chronic mental illness, were most distinctive in their adaptation. COPYRIGHT Society for the Psychological Study of Reporting Service 1990.

The Boolean operator AND *narrows* a search, as shown in the following Venn diagram *(mental illness* AND *homelessness* AND *Los Angeles).*

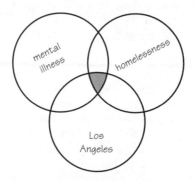

In contrast, the Boolean operator OR *enlarges* a search. As shown in the following diagram, a search for online data sources about the controversy over tribal rights in Indian adoption should use the term *Indian adoption* with the Boolean operator OR plus the term *Native American adoption* (that is, *Indian adoption* OR *Native American adoption).*

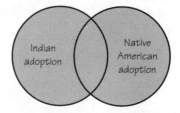

Boolean operators can also be combined. For instance, the student looking specifically for online information about Indian adoption in California could search with this command:

find keyword *Indian adoption* OR *Native American adoption* AND *California*

USING A TRUNCATION SYMBOL

A useful technique when using Boolean operators is to introduce a *truncation symbol.* Although different databases use different truncation symbols, the most common of these symbols are # and *. A truncation symbol stands for letters in a word, such that *adopt#* would stand for *adoption, adoptive, adopting,* as well as *adopt.* So, too, *legal** could stand for *legality* or *legalization.* The computer searches for any word beginning with the letters up to the truncation symbol. To be sure of finding all potentially relevant data sources, the student searching for online information about Indian adoption would use a truncation symbol; in the University of California's library catalog database, the symbol is #:

find keyword *Indian adopt#* **OR** *Native American adopt#*

EVALUATING INTERNET INFORMATION

Internet information can be found in a variety of formats, including gopher, file transfer protocol (FTP), newsgroups, and email discussion lists. However, when undergraduate students search the Internet, most now turn to the World Wide Web (WWW). Web search engines, such as Yahoo!, Lycos, and AltaVista, use Boolean operators to locate data sources, usually an overwhelming number of sources. While some of these sources may be excellent, others may be useless or distracting.

A good source of reliable demographic data, for example, is the Census Bureau's Web site at <http://www.census.gov>. Sponsored by the U.S. Department of Commerce, this site provides information about all kinds of population issues in various graphic and tabular formats, including maps and statistics. The site also provides downloadable software for census and survey processing, as well as access to the Census Bureau's online roundtables, which are forums for public comment.

Finding excellent Web sites usually requires sifting through the undigested lists provided by a search engine. For instance, a student writing about school uniforms as a deterrent to gang violence, and searching the Internet for potential data sources, was arbitrarily offered ten initial sites by the search engine AltaVista. These ten sites included links to the following range of sources:

- An editorial by Town Hall columnist William F. Buckley on "School Uniforms?!"
- An article in the *San Mateo Times* about a voluntary uniform policy for students in the Redwood City School District in California
- An illustrated catalog of "naughty" uniforms, supposedly accessible only to those over 18 years old, from a company in England selling "erotic goodies" over the Internet
- A White House press release, *"Manual on School Uniforms"*
- A state-by-state tabular summary of school uniform and dress code policies from the national nonprofit organization, Education Commission of the States
- Personal email from a spokesperson for the Policy Support Program in San Francisco

CRITERIA FOR ASSESSING WEB PAGES

Clearly, filtering out useful from useless information on the Internet is essential. We recommend applying the following five criteria for assessing Web pages:

▶ **1. Credibility of Local Origin.**   Where does the information come from? Before you link to a WWW data source, check its electronic address (its uniform resource locator or URL). If the address includes the abbreviation *edu* or *gov* (which identifies its association with an educational institution or government agency), you may find more reliable information there than if the source's URL has the abbreviation *org* (organization) or *com* (commercial). Other less common abbreviations, such as *net*, also exist.

EXAMPLES:

<http://www.census.gov/>   (the U.S. Census Bureau)

<http://www.soc.qc.edu/>   (the Sociology Department at Queens College, CUNY)

<http://www.aclu-sc.org/>   (American Civil Liberties Union of Southern California)

<http://www.cybergrrl.com/>   (the Cybergrrl Webstation)

We are *not* suggesting that organizational or commercial Web sites are automatically inferior. The American Civil Liberties Union of Southern California, for instance, provides texts of legislation, starting with the Bill of Rights, and updates about the progress of pending legislative initiatives from the organization's liberal point of view. Similarly, the Cybergrrl Webstation sponsors and houses SafetyNet, an excellent source of extensive data about domestic violence resources such as shelters. It also houses and sponsors WomenSpace, a shop-at-home pharmacy for women's products. However, you should be aware of any source's origin and judge its reliability.

▶ **2. Accountability.**   Is there an author or sponsor identified on the Web page, with an email link? Is there a link on the page back to its "home"? Useful sources provide this information about their data.

▶ **3. Timeliness.**   When was the Web page last updated? Is the information still accurate? Online information quickly becomes obsolete.

▶ **4. Scope and Coverage.**   Does the information on the Web page seem well researched? Are useful links embedded in the page? How does the online information compare with what you have found on paper? Are the graphics worth the time it takes to download them? Be a thoughtful consumer of online information and beware of electronic junk mail.

► **5. Reputation.** Is the Web page listed in any of the selective WWW search engines (for instance, FeMiNa for women's issues)? Check general search engines to see what other pages, if any, link to the Web page.

WEB SITES OF USE TO SOCIOLOGISTS

Although the World Wide Web has tremendous potential for information retrieval, the massive quantity, the uneven quality, and the haphazard organization of information limit its usefulness. Nonetheless, there are many useful Web sites for sociologists, including those listed here. (Because there is fairly rapid turnover among Web sites, some may have expired or changed their address by the time you try them.)

GENERAL INFORMATION

Lists of libraries with Web sites:
<http://www.yahoo.com/Reference/Libraries/>
<http://sunsite.berkeley.edu/Libweb/>
Library of Congress (in which all copyrighted books are deposited):
<http://lcweb.loc.gov/homepage/lchp.html>

Sociology and Related Social Science

Yahoo!'s sociology page (a gateway to other Web sources and a search engine):
<http://www.yahoo.com/Social_Science/Sociology/>
A Sociological Tour through Cyberspace:
<http://www.trinity.edu/~mkearl/index.html>
Research Engines for the Social Sciences:
<http://www.carleton.ca/~cmckie/research.html>
U.S. Census Bureau:
<http://www.census.gov>
WWW Virtual Library (Sociology):
<http://www.w3.org/pub/DataSources/bySubject/Sociology/Overview.html>
Worldwide Sociology Resources:
<http://sosig.ac.uk/Subjects/sociol.html>
UCLA's Internet Techniques in the Social Sciences:
<http://www.sscnet.ucla.edu/css96.htm>
SocioWeb (a general compilation of information and links about sociology):
<http://www.socioweb.com/~markbl/socioweb/>

Sociology Cases Database Project:
    <http://www.nd.edu/~dhachen/cases/>
General Social Survey Resources (programs and data may be
    downloaded; surveys are available for the years 1972–1993; a
    searchable index of papers utilizing GSS data includes full
    citations and short abstracts):
    <http://www.soc.qc.edu/QC__Software/GSS.html>

6

THE TEXTUAL
ANALYSIS PAPER

You may be assigned a paper asking you to analyze a book or portion of a book—for example, Max Weber's *The Protestant Ethic and the Spirit of Capitalism* or Erving Goffman's *The Presentation of Self in Everyday Life.* We call this method "textual" analysis because the text itself, what the author wrote, provides your data. Your paper is *about* the text itself, not about the text's subject matter. For example, a textual analysis of Durkheim's *Suicide* might concern his theory of suicide or his use of statistical data to study suicide, not suicide itself. Of course, one could write a paper about suicide based on Durkheim's book, but it would be a different kind of paper, not a textual analysis paper. Your paper is an "analysis" because you take the author's work apart to examine the different components and then put them back together. This activity is called "explication"; a textual analysis explicates, or explains, what the author's main points are and how they are connected, and offers a critique of the author's argument. An analogy would be taking a car engine apart, explaining each part and how the parts work together, and evaluating whether the car is a good buy or a lemon.

Mastering the skill of explication will help you write better papers when a textual analysis is assigned. But, perhaps as important, this skill will help you evaluate more clearly all the books and articles you encounter in your academic career.

ASKING QUESTIONS ABOUT THE TEXT

In textual analysis, the text is not only your data but also the source of your question. That is, your question will arise from the author's ideas and arguments presented in the text and from your analysis of them. Your question is a vehicle for conversing with the author about the thesis or argument of the work. This conversation should be conducted in an analytically critical manner, which means that to carry on your end you must raise questions about the logic of the argument, the type and credibility of the evidence, the soundness of the conclusion, and the fundamental assumptions on which the argument rests.

Your assignment may specify how you are to analyze a text, or the format may be left up to you. Here are three main areas generally addressed in a textual analysis:

1. **Summary.** What is the author saying? This is the basic question in textual analysis. It involves considering the author's main point(s). In general, most people should agree on what the author is saying. Sometimes an instructor will assign a paper asking no more than this. He or she only wants students to demonstrate that they comprehend what the author is saying. But sometimes summary is not as easy as it seems. It requires seeing the forest and not just the trees, the entire book or article, not just the particular facts that are presented to support an argument. For example, Durkheim's *Suicide* is not just about the relationship between religious denominations and suicide; it is also about how social structure helps explain what is commonly considered the most private of individual acts, taking one's life.

To see the whole picture of a book or an article, study carefully any preface, introduction, or conclusion, and the first and last chapters of a book or first and last sections of an article. Read through and think about the table of contents. What is the point of having the chapters organized the way they are? Why do the first chapters come first? Read through the section headings of the entire book or article. They usually give important clues about what the author thinks is important. They are like signposts along a highway that tell you the cities you are going through.

How does this author deal with one important sociological concept or issue in this text? Rather than analyzing all the ideas that the author presents, in this approach you focus in depth on one significant aspect of the text. If you are reading Talcott Parsons's book on the *Evolution of Societies,* for example, you might ask how Parsons views modern society. In that case, your questions would include: "How does Parsons define 'modern society'? Why, in light of the overall purpose of the book, does he discuss modern society? What evidence does he use to support his claims about it?"

2. **Analysis.** Analysis involves going beyond what the author says. It means looking at relationships: relationships between evidence and conclusions, relationships between concepts in the text, and relationships between the concepts in the work being analyzed and other texts.

What devices does the author use to convince the reader that he or she is correct? One of the general skills students should learn in college is to analyze the devices that authors—all authors, not just sociologists or academic writers—use to convince a reader. All of these have their place in writing, but all can be misused. The key here is to learn to identify what an author is doing to persuade the reader to his or her conclusions.

Logical reasoning. The most common form of logical reasoning is the syllogism (an *if . . . then* statement). Here the author seeks to convince you that there is a logical connection between something you already believe and something he or she wants you to believe. For example, Durkheim essentially argues that if social groups have an effect on whether a person feels a moral wholeness and if moral wholeness influences whether a person might commit suicide, then there must be a relationship between social groups and suicide. Logical reasoning can also take the form of an analogy, in which something the author wants you to understand in a certain way is compared to something you are familiar with. For example, Durkheim argues that suicide is a form of deviance, just as crime is a form of deviance. Both stem from a sense of normlessness or "anomie." There are many other logical devices that authors use, but they all have in common that the authors' arguments *make sense.* They are *logical.*

Anecdote. Anecdotes are little stories used to illustrate a point. They are especially common in journalistic accounts. A journalistic account of crime would begin with a story about a particular criminal or crime victim, with the unstated assumption that this story is representative of all criminals or victims. A single statistic can be used anecdotally to add credence to a paper. Anecdotes can make a paper "come alive" and hold the reader's interest, but do not substitute for systematic evidence.

Appeal to authority. It is quite common to show that someone the reader respects agrees with the author's perspective. This can be either an "expert," whose knowledge of a subject qualifies him or her for respect, or an elite, whose social status or position makes the person believable.

Controlled study. This type of book or article is intended to answer a very specific and empirically verifiable question, such as "Are Catholics still less likely to commit suicide than Protestants?" A study designed according to the rules of the scientific method is conducted for this purpose. Durkheim rests his case on a controlled study comparing suicide rates in Protestant and Catholic areas of Europe.

Rhetorical virtuosity. This includes a number of devices that can be employed to convince a reader by way of the writer's skill at using language. A well-turned phrase or metaphor may sound poetic due to its selection of words (for example, baby boom, sensuous sixties, animal rights, or law and order). Scientific jargon can give unscientific ideas the sound of authority. Big words or convoluted sentences can make the author sound intelligent and knowledgeable. Humor, satire, or irony can be used to make opposing views sound ridiculous.

What is important is that the student understand what the author is doing, to be able to analyze the devices being used.

3. **Evaluation.** How well does the author answer his or her question and verify that answer? This is the realm of criticism (both positive and negative). It logically comes last. You can't really judge a text until you fully comprehend what the author is doing and how he or she does it. Evaluation is also the most subjective stage. While an instructor can grade how well you summarize or analyze a work, what you think of the work is your personal opinion. There may be disagreements about evaluation, but ultimately your opinions are your own. However, the line between analysis and evaluation is sometimes fuzzy, and an instructor may legitimately fault you for basing your evaluation on inaccurate summary or sloppy analysis. Instructors also have different tastes concerning how much evaluation they want. Some want students to express their opinions about a text, others just want summary and/or analysis. Evaluation involves asking the following questions:

Is the argument of the text clear? Is it clear what question the text is attempting to answer? Are the definitions precise and unambiguous? Are the concepts appropriate to the questions addressed? Are the conclusions explicitly presented or scattered throughout? This dimension of evaluation concerns the summary. If the summary is easy to do, the text rates highly on this criterion.

Does the author make valid assumptions? Identifying and evaluating an author's assumptions are two of the intellectual skills often demanded in sociological theory classes. Authors necessarily make assumptions about the way the world works. For example, some theories assume that human beings act primarily on the basis of material self-interest, whereas others assume that people are motivated by the need for social approval. Some theories treat society as the aggregation of individuals, assuming that all social behavior should be reduced to individual behavior. Others assume that there are factors such as social class that can only be understood at the given level of society. Evaluating such assumptions means identifying the author's assumptions to see how plausible they are.

How well does the text use evidence? Is the evidence adequate to the conclusions? If the text is based on a specific study, how well is it performed? If the evidence is less systematic, does it seem to be fairly drawn or carefully selected to favor the author's point of view? This is an area where many beginning students feel ill equipped because they have not been thoroughly trained in methods and may feel they don't know enough about a topic to gauge whether or not the evidence is selective. Some instructors, while admitting such limitations, encourage students to make a stab at this type of evaluation. Most students should have some sense of whether the evidence presented adequately supports the conclusion. One can ask, "Even if this evidence is true, does the author's conclusion necessarily follow?" You will find that the answer is often no.

Are the conclusions and implications supported by other works? There are times when we assume that other works have validity and therefore we compare the text being studied to other works. This is especially common where certain works have achieved a sort of "orthodoxy," at least by some sociologists. One might ask, for example, whether a work by a contemporary writer on deviance legitimately qualifies as a Durkheimian analysis.

Is the craftsmanship of the writing sound? Do the parts fit into a whole? Is the prose understandable? Do the ideas flow smoothly from one to another? Craftsmanship is basically the theme of this book. If you were grading the text according to the criteria we have set forth as good writing, how would that text stand up?

It is important to repeat that different instructors have different tastes concerning how much evaluation they want and along what criteria. Some want you to basically stick to the text itself. Others want the text evaluated relative to other works. Some emphasize an evaluation of the logic, others of the evidence, and still others of the assumptions. Make sure you understand the instructor's preferences.

COMPARE-AND-CONTRAST ASSIGNMENTS

If you are asked to compare and/or contrast two authors' works (or two works by the same author), you must start by identifying the common topic under consideration and use that as the basis for your question. How do these two works deal with an issue that is central to each?

Any or all of these three aspects—summary, analysis, and evaluation—may be relevant to the particular work you are considering. Before you decide which questions will form the basis of your paper, you must read the text—and you must read it in a special way. We recommend that you buy your own copy of the book you will be using, if it is affordable. You will then be able to mark it up.

HOW TO READ THE TEXT

Before developing your question, get to know the text. As you read, keep in mind three general tasks. First, you must *identify the main points* that are explicitly presented as parts of the argument. Second, you must *identify the author's hidden assumptions*—that is, what she or he takes for granted about how the world works, and does not question or bother to justify. These assumptions are like the principles of physics taken for granted in building an engine. Third, you must *evaluate* the text, asking, for example, in what ways the argument is not convincing. What are its problems? How could it be better? Evaluating the argument is like diagnosing which of a car's engine parts do not work and how they could work, or arguing that the whole thing should be junked and stating why.

In other words, as you read you must ask yourself and ask the text the same sorts of questions that you will address in your paper. Following is a more detailed description of the close reading required for textual analysis.

GETTING TO KNOW SOMETHING ABOUT THE TEXT

Here are some things you must find out in order to become acquainted with the text:

Who is the author? What is her or his background? This information is sometimes included in the introduction of the book. If there is no biographical information in the introduction, or if the information is insufficient to give you a picture of the author, there are resources you can use to find out the information.

The *Biography and Genealogy Master Index* contains a list of authors' names, followed by a list of references in which you will find biographical information. The reference book titles are abbreviated; consult the front of the book for the complete titles.

Information on well-known authors—for example, the founders of the discipline—might also be found in *Encyclopaedia Britannica, Encyclopedia Americana,* or the *International Encyclopedia of the Social Sciences.*

When was the text written? What was the social climate of the period? To determine when the text was written, look at the copyright date in the front of the book. If you find more than one date, the first one indicates the date of the original printing or first edition. To determine the historical period in which the text was written, look first to your introduction. If this does not provide adequate information, you can use the preceding sources, paying particular attention to the historical information given in entries on the author or the countries where the author lived.

What is the polemical context? That is, where is the text located in the ongoing debate on the question? To whom is the author responding? Sometimes the text will reveal the polemical context by explicitly contrasting the author's argument with other perspectives. This information may be found either in the body of the text or in the preface or introduction. Sometimes it requires reading between the lines, paying attention to how the author refers to other works — for example, by drawing contrasts between her or his position and that of others. If the polemical context is not obvious, look for other books or journal articles about the author or the subject of the text. Often scholars write critiques or commentaries on others' work, especially if it is considered controversial or exemplary. This literature can be found in the library. (See Chapter 7 for guidelines about specific references.) Remember, the reference librarian can help you locate sources to help you get the information you need to write your paper.

READING TWICE

Read the text twice, for different purposes.

First, read for the big picture—get a feel for the text's organization and content. The author has major points that you are looking for. These major points, in turn, are supported by minor points. Pay special attention to the author's introduction, often called a preface, or to a foreword, written by an expert in the field.

After you have completed this preliminary reading, focus on the kind of question you will be addressing in your paper. If your instructor has specified a question, now is the time to consider it carefully. Be sure you understand what information to provide, how deeply to analyze the work, and how much of your own opinion to give. If the assignment is more general, look back over the categories of questions we listed earlier and decide which approach you will take: Will you analyze the text as a whole? Would you rather focus on a particular concept or aspect of the argument? Or should you compare this work to another one?

With your question in mind, read the text very closely the second time through; this reading forms the core of your "data collection." Your goal is to understand the interconnected points that constitute the author's argument and to record these important points on note cards. Note-taking during this second reading is an important step toward writing your paper. We will deal with it in detail later in the chapter.

What are you looking for in this detailed reading? Look for the author's argument—that is, the question the author is trying to answer and the evidence she or he uses to answer it. The following questions will assist you in identifying the text's argument; that is, the author's main points and the assumptions hidden beneath them:

- What is the author's question? For example, in *Suicide*, Durkheim asks, "What are the social factors that help explain suicide?"
- What is the author's answer—that is, what provides the core of the argument? What answers have other scholars given? Durkheim argues that the degree of social solidarity within groups that people belong to affects how likely they are to commit suicide. Protestants were more likely to commit suicide (when Durkheim lived) because

Catholicism provided greater social solidarity. He was trying to demonstrate that psychological explanations that emphasized individual pathology were not sufficient.
· What evidence does the author offer to support this answer? Is the evidence logical or empirical or both? Does the evidence actually support the argument?
· How does the author get from point A to point B? How do the main points that you identified in your reading relate to one another?
· What are the assumptions? What does the author take for granted, points without which the argument could not be made? Some examples of fundamental assumptions are that people have free will, that our social order constitutes the normal state of affairs, and that free enterprise benefits everyone.

As you engage in this second reading, you may want to adjust your question. If you planned on analyzing the text as a whole, for example, you may now discover that for this particular paper that task is too broad. If you attempt to explicate a work that is too comprehensive, your analysis may touch on a little bit of everything but fail to cover anything in depth; the result will be a weak analysis. Conversely, you may discover that it is not possible to discuss one concept without analyzing the text as a whole, or to explain this text without comparing or contrasting it with another work. If your focus is too narrow, your analysis won't make sense. In any case, remember as you read to adjust the breadth of your questioning to the particular materials you wish to analyze.

TAKING NOTES

In textual analysis, you will find note-taking a valuable tool for gaining access to the author's argument. Taking notes is a personal skill that varies somewhat from student to student. You might take very detailed notes on separate note cards or simply outline the main points. Whichever method you use, check its effectiveness. For example, after you have read your text for the second time, ask yourself the questions in the preceding list. If you cannot answer them, you may need to read the text more closely or change your note-taking technique.

In general, you should paraphrase the original text when taking notes. This means you should boil it down and put it in your own words. (See Chapter 7 for tips on effective note-taking.) You should quote only in a few special instances:

1. When the original is worded so elegantly, memorably, or powerfully that you do not want to change its effect.

2. When you just can't paraphrase it and do justice to the meaning, even though you have tried.
3. When the original is provocative or unusual, and you want to borrow the prestige of the original author to run defense for yourself, in case your reader disagrees with this point. Our own epigraphs illustrate the power of a distinguished author's exact words to enhance an argument.
4. When you want to do an extensive analysis on one small passage (an exegesis).

When you want to use the author's exact words, be sure to mark them as a quotation on your note card so that you will properly cite the source in your paper. You must also document paraphrases (see Chapter 4).

ORGANIZING YOUR PAPER

Once you have read the text carefully and made notes on the most revealing passages, the next step is to outline your analysis and plan how to present it. The essay format is more suitable than the journal format for textual analysis (see Developing an Argument: Logic and Structure, in Chapter 1). Within the basic format there are a number of ways in which you can organize your paper. Here are three basic outline patterns you can use or modify:

I. *Organize the body of your paper into three main parts corresponding to the three main tasks involved in explication:*
   1. Summary: Your description of what the author is saying; the author's main points
   2. Analysis: Your explanation of what is behind the author's argument; for example, the polemical context or debate being addressed, the author's hidden assumptions, the author's evidence, implications of the author's points
   3. Evaluation: Your assessment of the strengths and weaknesses of the author's argument (How well do the main points fit together? How relevant is the evidence to the points being made? How convincing are the conclusions?)

II. *Organize the body of your paper into major points that assert what you believe is most important about the text:*
   1. In your introduction, identify the most important features and state your position. You might also want to state the positions of other scholars unless your assignment excludes the use of outside sources.

2. In the second paragraph (or section, in a longer paper), summarize one main point you want the reader to know in order to accept your point of view and provide detailed evidence from the text to support this point.
3. Do the same thing in the third and fourth paragraphs (or sections), presenting one more major point in each.
4. In your conclusion, restate your claims and summarize your points supporting them.

III. *Organize your paper around comparing and contrasting:* There are two basic patterns you can follow to compare and contrast two works:

PATTERN I	PATTERN II
A (1st author)	1 (1st Point)
1 (1st point)	A (1st author)
2 (2nd point)	B (2nd author)
3 (3rd point)	2 (2nd point)
B (2nd author)	A (1st author)
1 (1st point)	B (2nd author)
2 (2nd point)	3 (3rd point)
3 (3rd point)	A (1st author)
	B (2nd author)

WRITING YOUR TEXTUAL ANALYSIS

Generally, your goal is to answer in writing, in a logical and coherent way, the same questions you have been asking about the text as you read. A review of Developing an Argument: Logic and Structure (in Chapter 1) will help you in this task. A tip for developing a cohesive paper is to refer back to the questions you are answering as you write. They can serve as a guide in determining which information you need to make your point, and which is extraneous. Keeping your key questions in mind as you write and revise will keep you from wandering. Remember to identify the author and text in your opening paragraph.

When writing a research paper, you must follow a special set of formal conventions for documentation. For textual analysis, however, it is usually sufficient to indicate only in the first reference the publication date of the text you are using. Thereafter you may document quotations with the author's name and appropriate page number. When referring to an idea or argument found more generally throughout the text, the author's name alone, included in one of your own sentences (for example, "Elias states . . ."), will suffice. See pages 51–52 for illustrations of these special citation formats. Consult your instructor for clarification and for her or his preference.

A SAMPLE STUDENT PAPER

Lysa Agundez's paper was written for a course in culture and personality. The text she chose to analyze is Norbert Elias's *The Civilizing Process.* It was an appropriate choice because Elias's goal is to show how individual psyches and actions take the same shape as the social structure in which they occur. We selected Lysa's paper not only because it illustrates a concise summary of a complex sociological work, but also because of its gritty and interesting subject. Here Lysa attempts to show how Elias uses the sociological imagination to connect the most personal of experiences with large-scale social relations.

Lysa identified and designed her paper around two key issues in the text she analyzed. The format of her paper is, accordingly, a variation of the three-part essay format—in this case, a two-part format. Our comments on the pages facing the paper indicate how Lysa addressed the three questions we have recommended you consider in any textual analysis: What is the author saying (summary)? What devices does the author use to convince the reader that he or she is correct (analysis)? How well does the author answer his or her question and verify the answer (evaluation)?

Demonstrating a problem many students encounter, Lysa's summary is more complete than her analysis and evaluation. Follow both her well-written paper and our remarks to see the strengths of her work, and how it could be made even better.

OUR COMMENTS

Because of the length of her paper, Lysa includes a title page (as suggested in Chapter 5).

Norbert Elias on the Development of Civilization through
Repression of Instincts

Lysa Agundez
Sociology 134
Professor Heritage
March 23, 1990

85

"The nature of this essay" is a vague phrase, and its meaning is unclear. It would be more effective to say: "This essay will address the two most important aspects of Elias's work," or "I will address two important issues raised by Elias."

Note that Lysa plans to address only two issues. Nowhere is it carved in stone that the student *must* have three main points (unless, of course, the assignment specifically says so). Since Lysa has identified two truly key ideas, her paper will have enough substance.

The second paragraph begins Lysa's summary of the first point she intends to address. Her summary is longer and more complete than the analysis and evaluation sections that follow. Although this is a drawback to her paper, in the case of writing as complex as that of Elias, we give her credit just for being able to identify and describe his main points.

Lysa's paper should include a bibliography or reference page, including the publication information on both volumes. As you will see, this is a serious shortcoming of her paper.

While it is helpful to make it clear which ideas expressed are being attributed to Elias, it is a good idea to vary the form of attribution. The repetition of "Elias believes" in this paragraph could have been avoided by using "Elias argues," "Elias maintains," "Elias contends," or other phrases.

This paper will discuss the theories of Norbert Elias, who argues that the development of civilization involves a repression of instincts. The nature of this essay entails addressing two issues: (1) The stricter control of emotion and behavior developed following the Middle Ages; and (2) The relationship of shame and the structure of society. Then I will discuss Elias's distinctive contributions to investigation of the civilizing process.

Norbert Elias is a German sociologist, whose two-volume masterpiece is titled *The Civilizing Process.* The first volume, titled *The History of Manners,* is a complete presentation of basic attitude changes of European manners and morals. Examples include attitudes towards bodily functions, table manners, sexual behavior, and aggression. The second volume, titled *Power and Civility,* presents a thorough sociological analysis of the development of civilized behavior formed by the centralization of society.

The process of civilization, Elias believes, involved a progressively stricter control of emotion and habits of restraint which led to socially institutionalized frontiers of shame and emotional standards. Thus, the growth of civilization, Elias believes, involves the gradual intensification of instinctual repression over the centuries. In *The History of Manners,* Elias documents the gradual domestication of human affects and emotions from the Middle Ages to our days. His purpose is to show how the psychical make-up of modern men and women differs in significant ways from their ancestors. Compared to modern man, medieval people, Elias argues, were faced with few barriers to the acting out of affect, be that in the area of aggression, sex, at the dinner table, or in the bedroom.

To prove his point, Elias turns to various etiquette and manners books that have been steadily written and very widely read since the days of Erasmus of Rotterdam. Written mainly for members of European court society, these books exemplify right and wrong behavior. Systematically comparing their changing content over time, Elias takes them as guides to the changing life-styles and sense of propriety on the passing historical scene.

Lysa's use of these examples as evidence for her explication would be strengthened by citing their sources in Elias's text. In fact, with material as colorful as this, direct quotation would liven up the scholarly discussion and keep the reader's interest.

The quotation marks around "natural" are not necessary because the word is not being quoted or used ironically or in a special way.

Lysa does a good job of summarizing the advice offered in the etiquette books that serve as Elias's data. More direct quotations would provide the reader with a stronger sense of the materials he used to reach his conclusions.

It is acceptable to use language normally considered vulgar to describe a historical situation, especially if it is used in the text. Still, if it makes you uncomfortable, or you think it might offend your instructor, you can adopt a euphemism.

Many of the teachings of Erasmus's book of manners would be taken for granted by most children today. For example, medieval writers tell their readers in quest for refinements of manners that one should not gnaw a bone and then throw it back into the common dish, that diners should not wipe their nose on their hands or spit into the plate, nor poke in their mouth, nor scratch themselves while eating. These elementary rules were necessary for fifteenth-century feudal nobles, who, in fact, ate with their hands, threw bones to dogs gathered around the table, dipped their fingers in common dishes, and drank from a common goblet.

By the sixteenth century, however, the time of Erasmus, standards became gradually more demanding, and people more self-conscious of their public manners. As time went on, eating habits gradually became more refined. People began to use forks instead of searching with pieces of bread for chunks of meat in the common pot. They were taught that they should use their knives unobtrusively so as not to threaten their neighbors at the table.

Erasmus, in an effort to teach "civility" to the nobility and the aspiring bourgeoisie, did not limit his advice to table manners. With a lack of embarrassment that might seem gross to modern sensibilities, he attempted to teach his public the circumstances in which spitting, farting, urinating, or defecating in public might or might not be defensible.

Spitting, for instance, was a common "natural" bodily function in the Middle Ages. As a matter of fact, it was even considered a custom and was commonplace in the courts of feudal lords. The only major restriction imposed then was that "one should not spit on or over the table but under it" (I, p. 156). In the sixteenth century, people were provided with spittoons. And in our age, the "need" for spitting in public has been altogether abolished.

Farting in public also became prohibited over the civilizing process. In the Middle Ages, it was considered unhealthy to "hold back wind" (I, p. 130). It was better to be emitted with a noise than to be held back. Gradually, however, the feeling of embarrassment increased, and it was

"Polite etiquette guides" is redundant, since etiquette by definition involves politeness. Never use two words when one will do!

The contrast between the reader's stereotypical image of Versailles as a glamorous place and the graphic insight Lysa provides about the use of perfume stimulates a lot of reader interest.

In using "complementary movements," Lysa seems to be making a valiant effort to avoid repetitive use of "changes." Still, because "movement" implies a collective effort of some sort (particularly in sociology), it is somewhat confusing here.

In general, Lysa makes good use of the kinds of transitional words and phrases discussed in Chapter 3. In this case, "moreover" indicates to the reader that what she reports in this paragraph is additional information relevant to what was discussed in the one preceding.

Did you catch "conceled" as a misspelling of "concealed"? Always proof your final draft for spelling errors, which detract from your presentation and make your ideas more difficult to follow. If you are using a word processor, a spelling check can be done electronically. See Chapter 5 for tips on correcting misspellings in your final draft.

Since "threshold of shame" is a special term that conveys one of Elias's key concepts, it would be good to define or explain it here, to be sure the reader knows what it means and how it is being used.

instructed to calm your body by farting only while covering
the sounds with coughs, or, if one was in a holy place, to
press your buttocks together. By the eighteenth century,
farting, like spitting, was abolished.

People furthermore used to urinate and defecate in
public, and polite etiquette guides simply taught their
readers that one should avoid looking at people engaging in
these activities. Even in the Palace of Versailles, people
used to relieve themselves in corridors and on staircases.
As a result, a huge consumption of perfume at the court was
required to hide the offensive odors in the palace.

To Elias, these changes are not just curious: they
indicate basic changes in the ways human beings perceive
themselves and use their bodies in relation to those of
others. People now began to mold themselves and others more
self-consciously and deliberately than was the wont and use
of the Middle Ages. Much of what we now consider "second
nature" was the result of a century-long process of gradual
domestication. As external restraint against personal
emissions gave way to self-restraint, an "invisible wall"
gradually grew up between one human body and another.

Elias also documents complementary movements involving
sleeping habits and sexuality. Here, also, the public
became distinguished from the private sphere. In medieval
society it was quite normal for many people, even
strangers, to spend the night in one room and even to share
the same bed. Today, however, the bedroom has become
privatized and separated from the rest of social life.

Moreover, in the Middle Ages it was customary for guests
at a wedding to terminate the proceedings by undressing the
bride and groom who were then obliged to consummate the
marriage in the presence of the assembled company. By the
late Middle Ages, the custom gradually changed to the
extent that the couple was placed on the bed fully dressed.
After this period, sexual life was conceled and dismissed
behind the scenes altogether.

Elias argues that these examples of changes in sexual
behavior, along with those illustrating changes in standards
of self-restraint, mark the advance in the threshold of shame.

Note that, in contrast to the use of quotation marks around "natural" on page 89, their use with "primitive" and "civilized" are appropriate here, since Lysa is using the words to indicate certain analytic definitions of those terms.

This is where Lysa begins her summary of the second point she introduced in the opening paragraph. It is not covered as fully as the first one was.

Because of this quotation's length, Lysa has appropriately indented and single-spaced it.

Here is a good example of why it is important to include full publication information for references: when we went to look for more information on this quotation (in this case, to check on correct punctuation), we could not find it on page 8 of our copy of the second volume. Perhaps it is because Lysa used a different edition than we have, but, since no publication information is provided, we cannot tell for sure.

When Lysa claims that Elias's thesis is "convincing," it sounds like she is ready to begin an evaluation of the text. However, she continues her summary without giving the reader any evidence of *why* she believes the thesis is convincing. See the following page for tips on how she might evaluate the text.

Noting that restrictions of various kinds surround the
elimination of natural functions in many societies, both
"primitive" and "civilized," he concludes that the fears of
natural elimination and the feeling of shame and repugnance
in which it is expressed do not originate from a rational
understanding of the origins of certain diseases, as one
might think. Actually, our understanding of their dangers is
attained only in the nineteenth century, at a very late
stage in the civilizing process.

Elias argues that our feelings of distaste and shame are
based on changes in the ways people live together in the
structure of society. He discusses these changes in social
structure at length in *Power and Civility*, in which he
announces:

> . . . [T]he civilizing of conduct and the
> corresponding transformation of human consciousness
> and libidinal make-up cannot be understood without
> tracing the process of state formation, and within it
> the advancing centralization of society which first
> finds particularly visible expression in the absolute
> form of life. (II, p. 8)

Despite the cumbersome formulation, Elias's basic thesis
is unexpectedly simple and convincing: as society became
more centralized, individuals came into close contact and
began to exercise greater self-constraint—"more affect
control," in Elias's jargon.

For example, Elias believes feudal knights behaved like
powerful and uninhibited children. These knights vigorously
(and often violently) engaged in self-defense and self-
gratification, clearly demonstrating minimal manners. "What
was lacking," Elias observes of this impulsive personality,
"was the invisible wall of affects which seems now to rise
between one body and another, repelling and separating" (II,
p. 256). The courtiers who congregated later in absolutist
courts were far more careful types; relying now on central
royal authority for physical protection, they vied (rarely
violently) for influence and advancement. Consequently, the

Again, Lysa has used quotation marks correctly here, since "courtoisie" is a foreign word. (By the way, it might have been interesting if she had pointed out how it demonstrates the way the tips Erasmus provided became the basis for our idea of and word for "courtesy.")

But why does the phrase "invisible walls" also have quotation marks around it? If it is directly from Elias' work, there should be a citation for it.

By including the concept of "sociological imagination," Lysa is demonstrating her familiarity with basic sociological principles. However, she could apply the idea more fully here. "Sociological imagination" does not just mean using an imaginative approach to research. It involves relating individual experience to large-scale social structures and processes; Elias does this very well by connecting personal habits to the historical formation of a centralized political state.

To strengthen her paper, at this point Lysa could have begun an analysis of Elias's work, making clear the ways in which Elias goes about convincing the reader to accept his point of view. (He uses empirical data written during the time he's theorizing about.)

Lysa's evaluation of the text should follow her analysis. This is where she might tell the reader why she believes Elias's basic thesis is "convincing" (perhaps because the data are contemporaneous with social changes that are taking place in people's everyday lives). Alternatively, she might choose to criticize how Elias attempts to justify his argument. (She could, for example, question whether etiquette books, however "juicy" and graphic, are accurate representations of how people live: Would you consider "Dear Abby" books, one author's perspective on relations among those in a certain social class, reflective of *your* everyday life?)

Sometimes students neglect to include criticisms of work they are analyzing because they are afraid it will undermine the strengths pointed out in their papers. However, including Thomas's critique adds to Lysa's paper by showing she is aware of the intellectual discussion he has generated. Unfortunately, there is no citation for Thomas, so there is no way for the reader to judge his credibility or to further investigate his assessment of Elias.

Rather than expressing the author's personal feelings, the conclusion should bring the reader full circle by summarizing or drawing conclusions about the work being discussed or its significance.

feudal knights increasingly had to regulate their behavior
to secure protection and promotions.

Furthermore, crude feudal "courtoisie" was replaced by a
more exacting code as courtiers strived to maintain their
status, fending off the bourgeoisie below. The threshold of
shame and embarrassment rose and rational forethought
became a more important guide to conduct; bodily functions
hidden, spontaneous impulses suppressed, and more elaborate
proprieties established. Henceforth those "invisible walls"
were everywhere, creating private selves who anxiously
calculated their actions, thereby increasing self-control
over passions and emotions.

Elias's ideas are similar to those of other authors,
such as Sigmund Freud. So what makes for the distinctive
contribution of this book? It is Elias's true leap of the
sociological imagination when searching for data through
which this process might be documented; his use of
etiquette manuals was very creative, and his research was
very thorough. Even though his work was published forty
years after it was written, it is not at all outdated. In
fact, it is encompassing and stands complete today.

One might argue that Elias's focus is too narrow. Elias
chose to focus only on the transformation of people from
the Middle Ages to our times and has eschewed the occasion
for a comparative treatment of the subject. As Keith Thomas
(1978) has pointed out, Elias says next to nothing about
the world of Graeco-Roman antiquity in which a similar
process had surely taken place, even though the results of
that process were largely lost during the Dark Ages. There
is next to nothing in the book about other high
civilizations, such as those of Asia, in which one can
discern similar trends. But these are, after all, minor
matters. One can hardly reproach an author who has given so
much for not having written a world history of manners.

In conclusion, I was very happy that I got to work on
such an interesting topic. I think one can learn from
Elias's detailed method of research—looking in countless
manners books and presenting the material the way things
really happened and then giving a thorough sociological
explanation of civilization.

7

THE LIBRARY RESEARCH PAPER

A library research paper requires you to use the library in two ways: first, to refine the question that you will address in your paper (if the question hasn't already been assigned); and, second, to collect the information that you will use to support your paper's thesis. In order to prepare your paper, you must know how to ask a good sociological question (see Chapter 1). You must also schedule your time strategically (see Chapter 2). Scheduling your time is especially important with a library research paper because if your library doesn't have crucial books and articles, you will have to order them through a service (often free) called interlibrary loan. Interlibrary loan is a way to borrow books temporarily from other libraries. Your own college library can usually arrange for this service if you need to read material that is not in your library. But the interlibrary loan service takes time.

BEFORE YOU GO TO THE LIBRARY: CHOOSING A TOPIC

You often start a library research project not knowing much about your topic. How, then, do you begin to develop a good question?

First, you must select a general subject area—an area that is relevant to the concerns of your course and of interest to you. One way to find a topic is to skim your syllabus and course readings. Be sure to consider the entire syllabus, since a topic that will be discussed later in the course might be the basis for a good research question. Your instructor can help at this stage by letting you know if your topic is too broad or too far afield.

Next, even before going to the library, construct some provisional questions. For example, let's say you want to study the feminist movement in the United States. Ask yourself why this topic interests you. Your personal interest in a subject not only motivates you during the research and writing process; it can also guide you to ask a good question. Also ask yourself what specific aspect of the subject you want to investigate for this particular class assignment, and what specifically you want to know about it. In the case of feminism, for example, you may want to focus your research on differences in wages ("Are women's wages lower than men's?"), on power differences ("Why do unequal power relations exist between men and women?"), or on ways people learn to fill the gender roles expected of them ("How are males and females socialized to enact sex role stereotypes in their daily lives?").

Remember to maintain a sociological perspective on the subject. The examples given in the previous paragraph are sociologically relevant because they are concerned with differences between groups of people (men and women) and because they focus on patterned relationships in the social world. A review of Chapter 1 will help stimulate the sociological imagination you need to ask a good question.

Once you have narrowed your topic and begun to shape it into a question, and once you have blocked out tentative deadlines for the various stages in a library paper on a time grid, you are ready to go to the library.

USING THE LIBRARY TO REVIEW THE SOCIOLOGICAL LITERATURE

Begin your work in the library by getting an overview of the sociological research that has already been conducted on your question. (The following section on locating references will help you do this.) This overview of research published in books and journal articles is called "a review of the literature." ("Literature" in this sense, of course, has nothing to do with fiction and poetry.) "Reviewing the literature" in sociology involves discovering whether scholarly research has been published on the question you tentatively have in mind, how the question was formulated, and what answers have been suggested.

Reviewing the literature will help you in two important and interrelated ways. First, a review of the literature helps you to refine your question. How has the question been framed before? Has more than one plausible answer been suggested as a result of empirical or theoretical research?

As you fine-tune your question, remember that you must be able to find sufficient evidence to support the answer you will propose, and that it must be specific enough to be researchable within the time frame of your assignment. Second, reviewing the literature helps you to identify those books and journal articles that contain reports of research into the question you will address in your paper. The quality of your paper will depend on how thoroughly you locate such research; it is the "data" you will use to support your thesis. Once you locate relevant books and articles, you will take in-depth notes on them.

LOCATING SPECIALIZED SOCIOLOGICAL REFERENCES

The key to the library is the reference section, where you can get help from two sources: reference librarians and reference texts. The reference librarians are there to answer your questions and help you find the most appropriate books, articles, journals, and abstracts for your project. You can also consult a variety of reference texts on your own, especially two reference texts that are librarians' "trade secrets": *Guide to Reference Books* by Eugene P. Sheehy and *Sources of Information in the Social Sciences: A Guide to the Literature* by William H. Webb and Associates.

If your course textbooks include lists of "Recommended Readings," often located at the ends of chapters, you can start with those references, choosing suggested books and articles that seem most appropriate. Start with the most recently published sources because they include references to earlier works.

Be aware that, for a college research paper, unlike most papers for high school, you will be expected to consult articles in specialized professional journals. (An annotated list of journals and other resources used by sociologists is given at the end of this chapter.)

In addition to any references you find in your textbooks, you should begin your research with the following six library resources on which sociology students rely:

- Specialized dictionaries and encyclopedias
- Library catalog
- *Sociological Abstracts:* SOCIOFILE
- *Social Science Index*
- *Social Science Citation Index*
- Other computerized bibliographic sources

Specialized Dictionaries and Encyclopedias

These references explain key terms and concepts, and provide background information on the life and times of key historical figures:

Borgatta, Edgar F. and Marie L. Borgatta, eds. 1992. *Encyclopedia of Sociology.* New York: Macmillan.

Hoult, Thomas Ford. 1969. *Dictionary of Modern Sociology.* Totowa, NJ: Littlefield, Adams.

Mann, Michael, ed. 1984. *International Encyclopedia of Sociology.* New York: Continuum.

Mitchell, Geoffrey Duncan. 1979. *A New Dictionary of the Social Sciences.* New York: Aldine.

Sills, David L. 1968. *International Encyclopedia of the Social Sciences.* New York: Macmillan.

Theodorson, George A. and Achilles G. Theodorson. 1970. *A Modern Dictionary of Sociology.* New York: Crowell.

The advantage of beginning with specialized dictionaries or encyclopedias is that they can give you a quick overview of a subject. However, they are often not the most up-to-date sources.

Library Catalog

Use the catalog to find suitable books in your library. Library books may be identified on index cards in drawers. Or books may be listed on celluloid microfiches that you must read in special machines to magnify this information. Most likely, however, your library catalogs its books with a computerized system that displays this information on a screen; and with some computerized online systems you can print out your own copy of appropriate information. In all three cases, only the equipment changes; the books are organized in the same way—according to author's name, title, and subject.

Finding information by looking in the catalog under author and title is relatively straightforward. But if you look under a subject for books about your topic and don't find any information, it may be because the subject you are looking under is not an official subject category. For example, if your paper is on the implications of regulating handguns, and if you look in the catalog under the subject "Handguns" or "Handgun Control," you will not find anything. "Handguns" and "Handgun Control" are not official topics. In this case, you must consult a special reference book to find official topics, called "subject headings." This special reference book, a large, red multivolume set called *The Library of Congress Subject Headings,* is usually placed near the catalog. For example, if you look up "Handguns" in *The Library of Congress Subject Headings,* you will find these instructions: "See Pistols." If you look up "Handgun Control" in *The Library of Congress Subject Headings,* you will find "See Gun Control." You will also be told that "Works on legal aspects of gun control are entered under 'Firearms—Law and legislation'." Finding books by subject in the catalog often requires this kind of detective work in order to find the right subject heading ("Firearms—Law and legislation"). As another example, if you want to find books on fraternities, *The Library of Congress Subject Headings* tells you to look in the catalog under the official topic "Greek letter societies."

SOCIOLOGICAL ABSTRACTS AND SOCIOFILE

Sociological Abstracts is published both as a set of annual volumes and as a computer database under the name SOCIOFILE, which includes references to sociological publications since 1974. Ask your librarian if your library has the computer version. If it does, ask for help in learning how to use it. The computer version is much easier and quicker because you don't have to do a separate search for each year of publications.

Sociological Abstracts gives more than bibliographic information. It also provides abstracts of articles published in major sociological journals. (An abstract is a summary of an article.) Learning to use *Sociological Abstracts* will save you much time, since these summaries will allow you to decide whether the sources themselves are relevant to your topic. In this way you can weed some out without having to locate and read them.

► **Printed Version.** To use the printed version of *Sociological Abstracts,* follow these two steps:

Step One—Locate the index volume for a recent year. Here you will find subject headings. Under the headings will be references to abstracts. Each abstract has its own unique number. For example, under the subject heading of "Firearms" you will find the information shown in Figure 7-1. Jot down the number at the end of any references to abstracts that look po-

FIGURE 7-1

INDEX ENTRY FROM *SOCIOLOGICAL ABSTRACTS*

Firearms
    firearm availability homicide rate relationship, Detroit, Michigan; police
      statistics 1851–1986: 91Y2087
    gun ownership, white southerners, cultural explanations; 1984–1989 General Social Surveys; 91Y0624

---

tentially useful; for example, 91Y0624. These numbers are not page numbers. They are abstract numbers. Each abstract, in another volume, has its own number.

Step Two—Now look up the abstract by its number in a separate volume, which is usually shelved next to the index volume. This abstract will give a summary of the article and bibliographic information telling you where the complete article can be found. Papers delivered at conferences are also summarized in the abstracts. When using the abstracts, make sure you are aware of the sources of articles, since it may be very difficult for you to find papers that have been delivered at conferences and have not been published. For example, if your topic is on gun ownership, then you would look up the number 91Y0624 and find the abstract shown in Figure 7-2. The bibliographic information indicates that this article was published in the journal *Social Science Quarterly*, which is found in most libraries.

If you already have an author's name and want an abstract of the article, you can start looking in the index volume under authors' names, not subject headings (see Figure 7-3). Locating 91Y0624 is the same as in step two above.

It is helpful to go through the printed versions of these indexes by annual volume in order to become familiar with new published sources for your research. At the end of each year, a cumulative index is compiled that

FIGURE 7-2

TEXT ENTRY FROM *SOCIOLOGICAL ABSTRACTS*

---

91 = 1991
Y0624 = abstract number

91Y0624
> **Ellison, Christopher G.** (Dept Sociology Duke U, Durham NC, 27706), **Southern Culture and Firearms Ownership,** LM *Social Science Quarterly*, 1991, 72, 2, June, 267–283.

¶ Four potential cultural explanations for the relatively high levels of gun ownership among white southerners are examined: the subculture of violence, racial prejudice, ideological conservatism, & the sporting gun subculture. Analysis of data from the 1984–1989 General Social Surveys (base N = 3,332) reveals modest links between southern subcultures of racism & conservatism & firearm ownership, negligible support for the subculture of violence thesis, & no empirical support for the southern sporting gun subculture hypothesis. It is suggested that structural factors may mediate the links between southern cultural orientations & gun-owning behavior; however, better methodological techniques are needed before these mediating factors can be understood. 2 Tables, 32 References. Adapted from the source document. (Copyright 1991, Sociological Abstracts, Inc., all rights reserved.)

FIGURE 7-3
INDEX ENTRY FROM *SOCIOLOGICAL ABSTRACTS*

Ellison, Christopher G., 91Y0624,
91Y2307

---

you can refer to and save time by not having to search through each individual volume.

▶ **Computerized Version.** To use the computerized version of *Sociological Abstracts* (**SOCIOFILE**), check first with your instructor or librarian. We cannot tell you exactly what syntax you will need to use because there are different software "shells" for accessing SOCIOFILE. However, your instructor or librarian can help you get started.

If you looked up "firearms" in the computerized version, you would find that there are 193 items (at the time of this writing), more or less with the most recent items given first. An example is shown in Figure 7-4. Note that some software shells will print only some fields unless you ask for a complete display; others will allow you to select which fields you want displayed. Note, too, that some of the fields have little meaning to you, such as "NUMBER" or "STANDARD NO." If you are able to download this information onto a floppy disk or print it directly, we recommend doing so; otherwise make a note of the author(s), title, year of publication, and journal, and paraphrase the abstract in your own words.

SOCIAL SCIENCE INDEX

This valuable source of bibliographic information comes in both printed annual editions and a computer database. The *Social Science Index* identifies where and when journal articles on social science topics have been published. The back section of each volume identifies where you can find book reviews. However, the *Social Science Index* does not print these articles or give you any summary information about them. Instead, it tells you which issues of the journal to look in for the article itself. The information is abbreviated, and the abbreviations are explained at the beginning of each volume. You will also find titles of indexed journals at the beginning of each volume.

Whether you are using the printed or the computerized version, *Social Science Index* lists information about articles in two ways—by author's name and by subject headings followed by a list of relevant articles. You can therefore search for information in two ways.

If you know the author's name, look it up in the index by year to see what he or she has published. If you know the year of the publication,

FIGURE 7-4
TEXT ENTRY FROM SOCIOFILE

NUMBER: 96W23573
AUTHOR(S): Weisman, Carol S.
AFFILIATION: c/o Women's Health Issues-Elsevier Science Inc, 655 Ave
Americas New York NY 10010
TITLE: Armed by Fear: Self-Defense Handguns and Women's Health
PUB YEAR: 1995
JOURNAL: Women's Health Issues, 1995, 5, 1, spring, 3–7.
STANDARD NO: CODEN: WHISEH ISSN: 1049–3867
COUNTRY: United States
LANGUAGE: English
PUB TYPE: Abstract of journal article (aja)
ANNOUNCEMENT: Social Planning, Policy & Development Abstracts
(SOPODA), 018, 01,
1996
ABSTRACT: The gun industry has exploited women's fear of crime & created
a huge female market for self-defense handguns. The industry touts personal
firearm protection as the answer to crimes committed by violent strangers
lurking everywhere. Exploration of the real risks to women from injury &
death related to firearms shows that white females, the target market for
guns, are the least likely victims of violence by strangers; the threat for this
group is domestic violence. Statistical studies have shown that a gun in the
home is a significant risk factor in homicide. Gun ownership increases risks
from gun injuries, from one's own gun either accidentally or from suicide. If
domestic violence is a problem, husbands, intimate partners, & other
relatives also have access to the gun. Since a number of factors determine
how successfully a gun can be in thwarting a criminal intent, not just gun
ownership, owning a gun may not actually increase personal safety. 25
References. M. Pflum (Copyright 1996, Sociological Abstracts, Inc., all rights
reserved.)
IDENTIFIERS: women's personal safety; gun ownership; statistical studies;
SUBJECT HDGS: *Firearms (D303600). *Family Violence (D289200).
*Victimization (D902700). Fear of Crime (D294000). Violence
(D905400). Protection (D672200). Females (D296700).

---

simply get the index for that year and look up the author's name. The
listings are arranged in alphabetical order. For example, if you are looking for a source citation of an article written by Richard Kensic in 1992,
pull out the 1992 index and look under Kensic, Richard F. As you can
see in Figure 7-5, the information is abbreviated. By checking the abbreviations at the beginning of the volume, you will be able to establish
that Richard Kensic published an article, "Targeting a Los Angeles Street
Gang," on pages 50–51 in volume 59 of the journal *Police Chief* in March
1992.

You can also look under subject headings for issues and titles of articles connected with your topic. For example, if you look up "Gangs" in

FIGURE 7-5
AUTHOR'S NAME, *SOCIAL SCIENCE INDEX*

Kensic, Richard F.
Targeting a Los Angeles street gang, *Police Chief* 59:50–1 Mr '92

FIGURE 7-6
SUBJECT ENTRY, *SOCIAL SCIENCE INDEX*

Gangs
Street Corner Society revisited; special issue. *J Contemp Ethnogr* 21:3–132 Ap '92
Targeting a Los Angeles street gang. R. F. Kensic. *Police Chief* 59:50–1 Mr '92
Why pick on us? [yakuza gangs] R. Delfs. *Far East Econ Rev* 155:27 Mr 5 '92
Youth gangs: an essay review. I. A. Spergel. *Soc Serv Rev* 66:121–40 Mr '92

the index, you will find another reference to this same article, "Targeting a Los Angeles Street Gang," as shown in Figure 7-6.

SOCIAL SCIENCE CITATION INDEX

Like *Sociological Abstracts,* and *Social Science Index,* this valuable source of bibliographic information comes in both printed annual editions and a computer database. But the *Social Science Citation Index* gives other information and is a unique and invaluable reference source for established scholars and undergraduates alike.

Social Science Citation Index has three special features. First, it identifies the references that authors cite in their articles (hence, the word "citation" in its title). This feature allows scholars to trace the interconnected network of a research tradition and see which scholars' work influenced which other scholars. Second, this work enables scholars to find information by academic or corporate affiliation. These two features are used primarily by graduate students, researchers, and professors. However, the third unique feature of this reference source is particularly useful for undergraduates. Unlike the other reference works listed so far in this chapter, *Social Science Citation Index* does not list information about articles according to subject headings. Rather, *Social Science Citation Index* lists this information according to the keywords in these articles' titles.

Do not expect to find the *Social Science Citation Index* easy to decipher and read, because so much information, often abbreviated, is compressed into this source, and in the published version the print is quite small.

However, the following examples will help you understand its organization. And with some brief experience using it, you will find the *Social Science Citation Index* to be an indispensable reference tool.

Each annual set of the published version of *Social Science Citation Index* includes these four volumes:

- *Subject Index*
- *Source Index*
- *Citation Index*
- *Corporate Index*

However, undergraduates usually need to use only the first two volumes. To use *Social Science Citation Index* follow these corresponding two steps:

Step One—Look in a recent year's *Subject Index* to find articles that have words of interest in their titles. For example, if you are investigating the relationship between firearms and violence, you could look under "Firearms" or "Violence" to see if any articles were published in that year with those words in their titles. See Figure 7-7 for an example. From this

FIGURE 7-7

SUBJECT INDEX ENTRY, *SOCIAL SCIENCE CITATION INDEX*

FIREARMS
ACCESSIBIL	+ BRENT DA
ADOLESCENT	•
ATTITUDES	+ SLUDER RD
AUSTRALIA.	+ CANTOR CH
CASE	+ KIRBY A
CHILDHOOD	+ COPELAND AR
CONTROL	KIRBY A
CULTURE.	+ ELLISON CG
DENMARK.	+ THOMSEN JL
FATALITIES	COPELAND AR
	THOMSEN JL
HOMES.	BRENT DA
INJURIES.	+ CHRISTOF KK
INTRODUCTL	THOMSEN JL
INVESTIGAT.	•
KILLING	+ KASSIRER JP
LEGISLATION	THOMSEN JL
LOCAL	KIRBY A
NEW	THOMSEN JL
OFFICERS	SLUDER RD
OWNERSHIP	ELLISON CG
PATTERN	THOMSEN JL
PEDIATRIC.	CHRISTOF KK
PERCEPTIONS . . .	SLUDER RD
PRESENSE.	BRENT DA
PROBATION.	SLUDER RD
PUBLIC-POL	+ ZIMRING FE
REDUCING	CHRISTOF KK
RELATIONS	KIRBY A
ROLE	SLUDER RD
SOUTHERN	ELLISON CG
STATE.	KIRBY A
SUICIDE	CANTOR CH
SUICIDES	BRENT DA
THRESHOLD	KASSIRER JP
VIOLENCE	ZIMRING FE

list you could tell that such an article was indeed published during this year. It was written by F. E. Zimring.

Step Two—Look in the same year's *Source Index* under the author's name (F. E. Zimring) to find the complete bibliographic information. Figure 7-8 provides all the information you need to find the complete article. Zimring's article appeared in *Scientific American,* volume 265, number 5, 1991, on pages 24–30. The article included five citations, which are identified, as is the author's institutional affiliation (Law School, Berkeley).

OTHER COMPUTERIZED BIBLIOGRAPHIC SOURCES

In addition to using the computerized versions of library card catalogs, *Sociological Abstracts* (SOCIOFILE), and *Social Science Citation Index*, you may be able to search for Internet data if you have access, at school or at home, to a computer, a modem, and email. (See pp. 64–71 for a discussion of how to search for and judge online information.)

Finally, your library may have other computerized bibliographies that will suggest books and articles to read. While the library catalog lists books, these other sources list journal articles as well. Like SOCIOFILE, the computerized version of *Sociological Abstracts,* other academic disciplines have their own resources, such as PSYCHLIT (the computerized version of *Psychological Abstracts*), ECONLIT (the computerized version of *Economic Abstracts*), and ERIC (the Educational Resources Information Center, a national information system sponsored by the U.S. Department of Education that collects educational documents and makes them available to teachers, administrators, students, and other researchers). You can also consult computerized bibliographies on a variety of particular topics, such as CDB (the Chicano Database), PAIS (the

FIGURE 7-8

SOURCE INDEX ENTRY, *SOCIAL SCIENCE CITATION INDEX*

ZIMRING FE
- **FIREARMS, VIOLENCE AND PUBLIC-POLICY**
  SCI AM   *265(5):24-30*   *91*   **5R** **GP213**
    UNIV CALIF BERKELEY, LAW, BERKELEY, CA 94720, USA

(ANOM)	90 CRIME US VIOLENCE GUN
BAKER SP	IN PROCESS INJURY F ACT
NEWTON SD	89 FIREARMS VIOLENCE AM
WRIGHT JD	83 GUN WEAPONS CRIME VI
ZIMRING FE	87 CITIZENS GUIDE GUN C

Public Affairs Information Service), and POPLINE (for Population Information). Ask your librarian which of these are available at your college or university and for help on how to use them. They can be very useful for finding books and articles on the topic of your paper.

Selecting Information

The Information Age makes it possible to retrieve mountains of information through electronic wizardry. However, it is easy to become so overwhelmed by the quantity of information that you lose the capacity to evaluate the quality of information. Therefore, after you have done the preliminary work of locating bibliographic citations on a topic, and before you actually begin to record the information, you must sort through the potential sources and decide which ones are worth pursuing. (Of course, one doesn't finish searching for sources before recording information, but there is still the sequence of locating, sorting, and recording.) How do you dig through the mountain of sources to find the few nuggets that will enrich your library research paper?

The main principle is sociological: there are strong relationships between the quality of the information and the social setting of the source. Some journals and magazines, some book publishers, and some authors are more reliable than others. Most students would intuitively know that tabloid magazines are not appropriate for college research papers (unless they were the topic being researched), but they are an extreme example. In general, we can identify a few guidelines for choosing reliable sources:

- Academic journals are more reliable than popular magazines. Some academic journals, such as *American Sociological Review*, may be difficult for undergraduates to read, especially the articles with complex statistics. But you can get the gist of such articles and consult the bibliographic references at the end of the articles. Although popular magazines should not be excluded altogether, you should be critical of their contents.
- University presses are generally less likely to print poorly researched books than are commercial presses. For commercially published books, those written by academics are usually more reliable than those written by journalists. Again, the point is not to ignore books by journalists, but to approach them with a critical eye.
- Articles and books that carefully cite their sources of information are generally more reliable than those that don't. While some students find a heavily footnoted article or book daunting, carefully cited references provide the reader with the means to follow up on the author's assertions.

RECORDING INFORMATION

Index cards are a handy tool for gathering two kinds of information: bibliographic information on the sources you consult and the ideas you borrow from these sources.

Bibliography cards. Make one bibliography card for each source. Include on this card the following information in this order:

Author: all authors of the work with surnames and first names in inverted order

Title: article, chapter, or book

Facts of publication:

For journals: journal name in full, date of publication, volume number, inclusive pages

For books: city of publication, publisher's name, publication date

Take this list with you to the library so that the bibliography cards you write will be complete. You will need all the above information when you cite your sources later in your paper. So write down this information when it's easy to do so—that is, when you have the source in front of you—and avoid wasting valuable time backtracking. Later you will be able to shuffle these bibliography cards into alphabetical order, based on authors' surnames, and in this way prepare the list of references for your paper (see Chapter 4). A variation on the note card system is to use a looseleaf binder and looseleaf paper. This allows shuffling and ordering, just as index cards do. Software companies are also beginning to develop and market comparable programs, such as *3 × 5,* which can be used on a personal computer.

Note cards. You make note cards for two reasons: (1) to support your memory while thinking about a topic and (2) to shape data into usable form. The physical act of recording on cards loads the data into your mind very efficiently, so that you can retrieve them in manageable chunks as you consolidate your answer to your research question. Note cards also help you avoid problems of parroting and unintentional plagiarism. Parroting means mechanically repeating sources without any sign of your own thinking; for information about the serious offense of plagiarism, see Chapter 4.

Limit each note card to one piece of information from a single article or book. You may quote exact words from the original, or you may paraphrase the ideas. "Paraphrase" means summarize the idea in your own words (see Chapter 4). *Remember to include specific page references* to words and ideas that you record on your note cards as you write them. You will need this information later.

Look for two kinds of information to record on note cards: (1) main concepts related to your research question, and (2) any particularly interesting supporting details. "Interesting" means interesting to you—details that stick in your mind as you read because they connect with your own academic or personal experience.

Label each note card with a subject heading of your own at the top. Try to come up with a description that is precise without copying out the whole note again. You will depend on these subject headings later to group your note cards and sort them into piles. These piles will be the basis for a provisional outline for your paper. At the bottom of each note card, identify the source of your borrowed idea. You can abbreviate this information on a note card because you already have a complete record on a bibliography card. Remember to include the specific page number.

What exactly are you looking for in your note-taking? In some ways, you can think of this part of your work as asking questions not unlike those you would pose in a textual analysis (see Chapter 6). Your notes should indicate answers to the key questions about the article or book you are reading: What major question is the author addressing in this work? Why does the author think the question is important to sociological theory or to the world at large? What methods did the researchers use to try to answer the question and/or what work of others is cited to make a significant point? What thesis does the author propose in response to the question? What evidence does he or she use to support the answer?

As you take notes you will see that there is no one answer to your research question. It is not a matter of finding the truth, but of tracing the main issues raised in regard to the question, the main answers proposed, and the main disagreements among those engaged in the field. Eventually you will use these notes to explain in your paper why you believe one answer to be more convincing than the others that have been suggested.

When you first start your project you may find yourself making quite a few note cards because the subject is often new to you. However, as you read more, and become more informed, you will be narrowing down the answer to your question. At the same time your thesis will be emerging more clearly in your own mind, and you will be selecting subsequent readings more deliberately. As the material becomes familiar you will likely take fewer notes per reading. This process of adjustment and refinement happens almost automatically.

Here is an original passage from Emile Durkheim's book *Suicide* (1951). See Figure 7-9 for a sample note card based on the passage:

As a rule suicide increases with knowledge. Knowledge does not determine this progress. It is innocent; nothing is more unjust than to

FIGURE 7-9
A SAMPLE NOTE CARD

Subject heading label identifying noted idea	relationship between suicide & knowledge
Borrowed ideas recorded as part quotation/ part paraphrase	"suicide increases with knowledge" but is not caused by knowledge They both result from loss of religious faith.
Bibliographic information identifying source	Durkheim 1951, p. 168

accuse it. . . . But these two facts result simultaneously from a single general state which they translate into different forms. Man seeks to learn and man kills himself because of the loss of cohesion in his religious society; he does not kill himself because of his learning. It is certainly not the learning he acquires that disorganizes religion; but the desire for knowledge wakens because religion becomes disorganized. Knowledge is not sought as a means to destroy accepted opinions but because their destruction has commenced. (P. 168)

Remember to include on your note cards the page number(s) for both quotations and paraphrases. Otherwise you may later have to skim the entire source just to locate the page for a passage you want to cite.

LOOKING DEEPER

Now that you are immersed in your topic, you can use the materials that you have found to direct you to further books and articles that may be useful to you. As you are engaged in taking notes, make bibliography cards for any references in your reading that seem relevant to your topic. You may discover these in the body of the work itself or in the list of references at the end. The library catalog (for books) and serials list (for periodical literature such as journal articles) will help you in locating these references in your library.

ORGANIZING YOUR INFORMATION

Once you have finished making note cards, reread them in any order to get an overview of the information you have gathered on your topic. You should now be able to state your thesis, which these notes support, very clearly. With your thesis in mind, sort your note cards into piles, according to the subject headings you gave them. This shuffling will not necessarily be neat, but it should help to separate main points and prepare the basis for an outline.

MATCHING THESIS, NOTE CARDS, AND OUTLINE

Decide on the main point in each pile of note cards and make that a main point in your outline. Use the detailed information in the pile to elaborate on this main point.

You may find that some of your note cards no longer fit the final version of your thesis. If so, abandon them. Including irrelevant information, even though you worked hard to get it, will distract your reader, weaken your argument, and count against you.

In order to decide on a sequence of main points—that is, which main point to start with and what order to follow with the others—think of your reader. What order will be the most convincing? What order of main points will best support your thesis? Then use each main point as the basis of a different paragraph. Use details from your piles of note cards to build up each paragraph, presenting your sequence of thoughts in a logical pattern with transitions marking the movement of your argument (see Chapter 3 for more information on transitions).

But don't rely on the piles of cards to "write" the paper for you. They should be used to illustrate and substantiate the points that you are making from your own ideas. They should only be the facade that goes on your own basic structure. Make a basic plan or outline for the paper with your own ideas, using what you learned from reading, but do not use your note cards as a crutch. Sometimes papers seem more like a collection of sentences from index cards than a smoothly flowing, logically structured paper. If you are worried that your library paper seems to be an inferior patchwork of other people's ideas, then insert your own judgment: make inferences from your borrowed material, connect the borrowings explicitly to the points they are supposed to illustrate, or editorialize on their meaning. In the concluding section, summarize your major findings. Here you can also briefly refer to other related issues or topics that merit further investigation.

JOURNALS OFTEN USED BY SOCIOLOGISTS

Scholars rely on journal articles, as well as books, to keep up with new research and professional opinion. But journals aren't a trade secret. Undergraduates, as apprentice scholars, can also use journal articles. Most college libraries have a quiet, convenient place where current issues of major journals are kept before being bound and shelved, like other books, in the main sections of the library. We recommend that you find this reading area, often called "Current Periodicals," and browse through some of the journals in the following list. This experience will give you a dramatic sense of the discipline's ongoing research tradition, which is only hinted at in textbooks. It may also trigger some ideas about possible topics for your future papers. Although the articles in these journals are intended primarily for a trained scholarly audience, rather than the general public, and sometimes employ sophisticated statistical techniques, you will find many articles easily accessible to undergraduates.

American Journal of Sociology: Published bimonthly by the University of Chicago Press, this influential journal includes theoretical and research articles, book reviews, and commentaries on articles published previously.

American Sociological Review: Published bimonthly by the American Sociological Association (ASA), this review covers diverse areas of sociology, often with a statistical and empirical orientation. A cumulative index appears every three years.

Annual Review of Sociology: These review articles, which summarize some particular field of sociology, reflect a broad perspective and can be found under such categories as differentiation and stratification, institutions, political and economic sociology, social processes, policy, historical sociology, urban sociology, and political sociology.

British Journal of Sociology: Published quarterly, this journal discusses historical, theoretical, and methodological issues. An annual index includes book reviews.

Contemporary Sociology: Published bimonthly by the ASA, its special feature is to review books, journals, articles, and films that cover a wide range of areas, such as historical and comparative sociology, social psychology, gender, education, and stratification. The review essays are especially useful for learning about new publications and sociologists' evaluations of them.

Criminology: Published quarterly, this interdisciplinary journal emphasizes research about crime and deviant behavior within the social and behavioral sciences and presents articles on the theoretical and historical components of crime, law, and criminal justice.

Demography: This interdisciplinary journal, published quarterly by the Population Association of America, includes research studies on developing countries as well as on developed countries.

Gender and Society: Published quarterly, this interdisciplinary journal is sponsored by Sociologists for Women in Society. It aims to advance the study of gender, as well as racial, ethnic, cultural, and national diversity.

Journal of Aging Studies: This quarterly publication highlights innovative research approaches and critiques of existing theory and empirical work related to age and aging.

Journal of Contemporary Ethnography: Published quarterly, it presents ethnographic studies based on qualitative interviewing and participant observation.

Journal of Health and Social Behavior: Published quarterly by the ASA, it uses a sociological perspective in understanding health-related issues; for example, organizational aspects of hospitals or class characteristics of sufferers from various illnesses.

Journal of Marriage and the Family: Published quarterly by the National Council on Family Relations, it covers such diverse research areas as family planning, family structure, theories of the family, and cross-cultural studies on fertility. Each issue also features a book review section.

Journal of Personality and Social Psychology: Published monthly by the American Psychological Association (APA), this journal is divided into sections on attitudes and social cognition, interpersonal relations and group processes, and personality processes and individual differences.

The Journals of Gerontology: Published bimonthly by the Gerontological Society of America, this interdisciplinary journal seeks to promote the scientific study of aging and the life course.

Qualitative Sociology: This quarterly journal publishes research based on qualitative research methods, such as interviewing, participant observation, ethnography, historical analysis, and content analysis.

Sex Roles: A Journal of Research: Published bimonthly, this journal presents empirical and theoretical examinations of the underlying processes of gender role socialization.

Social Forces: Published quarterly, this journal for social research and methodology presents articles on such topics as mobility, class, ethnicity, gender, and education. Each issue includes book reviews.

Social Problems: Published five times yearly, this is the official journal of the Society for the Study of Social Problems.

Social Psychology Quarterly: Published quarterly by the ASA, it covers empirical and theoretical studies related to social interaction, socialization, labeling, conformity, and attitudes.

Sociological Focus: This quarterly journal, sponsored by the North Central Sociological Association, presents articles of general interest to sociologists.

Sociological Forum: This official journal of the Eastern Sociological Society, published quarterly, contains articles that link subfields of sociology to other disciplines.

Sociological Inquiry: Published quarterly for the chapters of the Alpha Kappa Delta (the Undergraduate Sociology Honors Society), it covers a wide range of sociological topics.

Sociological Methods and Research: Published quarterly, it covers research in qualitative and quantitative methodological issues in the field of sociology. It also includes review articles.

Sociological Perspectives: Sponsored by the Pacific Sociological Association, the purpose of this quarterly journal is to advance research and theory in sociology and related disciplines.

Sociological Quarterly: Sponsored by the Midwest Sociological Association, this journal presents research on recent theoretical, methodological, and empirical developments in the field of sociology.

Sociological Review: Published quarterly in England, this interdisciplinary journal presents a range of sociological topics, such as social mobility and class structure, and includes book reviews.

Sociological Theory: A semiannual publication of the ASA, it is devoted to discussions of new and old sociological theories, theory construction, and theory synthesis. The journal also includes a section for debate and comment on recent theoretical controversies.

Sociology: This quarterly journal, which is the official publication of the British Sociological Association, covers the full spectrum of areas in sociology.

Sociology of Education: Published quarterly by the ASA, this journal contains papers on human social development as well as on relations among educational institutions.

Symbolic Interaction: Published quarterly by the Society for the Study of Symbolic Interaction, this specialized journal presents empirical and theoretical articles that take a symbolic interactionist perspective.

The preceding list of periodicals related to sociology is not exhaustive. For more references to specialized journals and governmental sources, ask your reference librarian or consult this useful book:

Bart, Pauline and Linda Frankel. 1986. *The Student Sociologist's Handbook.* 4th ed. New York: Random House.

8

THE ETHNOGRAPHIC FIELD RESEARCH PAPER

In an *ethnographic field research* project, your data come from observing or interacting with people in everyday social settings, which are known as "the field." The data are gathered through observation when a researcher visits the setting, participates in the setting's activities (called *participant observation*), and/or interviews participants in the setting.

GOALS AND METHODS OF ETHNOGRAPHIC FIELD RESEARCH

1. Ethnographic field research sets out to represent as accurately as possible the process of social life *from the point of view of the participants* (or "members") in the field setting being investigated. Since a scientific hypothesis is an explanation of social processes proposed by someone *outside* the research setting, the ethnographic researcher does not engage in the testing of hypotheses. However, some sociologists do engage in field-work to test hypotheses about what happens in social settings or why it happens. This kind of fieldwork, which we refer to as "structured field research," is discussed in Chapter 9.

2. The ethnographic researcher usually conducts research by closely observing what people are doing, by talking with them informally, and often by participating in activities with them. If interviews are conducted, the ethnographer uses questions that encourage respondents to answer in their own ways and with their own words. The choice of methods used

115

in ethnographic research depends on the characteristics of the setting and its inhabitants and on the personal style of the researcher.

Unlike most deductive researchers, then, the ethnographic field researcher does not use a predesigned research instrument, such as a written questionnaire. And unlike the structured fieldwork described in Chapter 9, ethnographic field research rarely involves quantitative measurement. While predesigned and quantitative methods are useful for measuring some aspects of the social world, they do not convey the intricate and subtle transactions that the ethnographer seeks to understand.

3. Reports based on ethnographic field research—called *ethnographies*—often produce new theoretical insights, but they are most distinctive for their vivid descriptions of actual social scenes and transactions. In other words, even after collecting data, the ethnographer typically does not attempt to propose a hypothesis about *why* something happens in the social world. Instead, ethnographic research attempts to uncover *what* happens in a social setting, *how* social relationships are conducted, and *what* those events and relationships mean to those involved.

In doing ethnographic research, your sociological imagination is exercised by the opportunity to see society's institutions, such as the police, the judicial system, and the health care system, as they are actually enacted in the personal lives of specific individuals. Because it takes sociology out of the classroom and into the "real world," and because it allows you to view the world through the eyes of people often very different from yourself, an ethnographic field research project can be especially challenging and exciting.

ASKING AN APPROPRIATE QUESTION

Often the goal of your research project will be specified by your instructor. Ethnographic research assignments frequently ask you to do one of the following:

1. Look at social interaction in your everyday life—among family members, friends, fellow students, or co-workers, for example—in new ways. The goals are to describe patterns and processes that often pass unnoticed in your daily interactions and to use your sociological imagination to relate these personal patterns and processes to specific course concepts. This kind of project might ask you, for instance, to talk to fellow students about their relationships with friends; to observe how those in your dorm, apartment, or family deal with odd behavior; or to watch

how individuals attempt to present a certain impression of themselves to others.

2. Visit a setting selected by your instructor, in which social activities of special concern in your course occur, and investigate how those present carry out routine activities and make decisions. Examples of this kind of assignment are going on a police ride-along, attending traffic or small claims court, or interviewing a mental health professional.

In some classes, however, you may have to develop your own question to address through ethnographic research, or you may simply be assigned to visit a setting of your choice and describe what it is like. If so, remember that, unlike much other sociological research, the goal of ethnographic field research is not to determine what causes some social event or relationship. Therefore, avoid devising a research question that asks *why* something happens in your research setting. Instead, concentrate on asking *what* (for example, "What does a police officer do during his or her time on the job?") or *how* (for example, "How do those sharing an elevator ride deal with one another in the limited space available?"). In the sample student paper at the end of this chapter, the author addresses this question: "*How* does a judge decide whether or not to recommit a psychiatric patient against his or her will?"

Here are the kinds of "what" and "how" questions that will point your ethnographic research in the right direction: What do people do in this setting? How do they explain what they do? What kinds of things interest and concern them? How do group members work together to accomplish a task? How are new members taught the values and procedures common to the setting? What do group members mean by any special words they use?

REVIEWING THE LITERATURE

In a deductive research process, a review of relevant research done on the same topic is used to develop a hypothesis for testing through data collection. However, because the kind of fieldwork we are describing here does not involve hypothesis-testing, instructors assigning ethnographic research projects often do not require that you summarize the literature on the question you are investigating.

Nevertheless, your instructor, in order to encourage you to become familiar with work already done on the question you are investigating, may prefer that you give an overview of relevant research on your subject. Or you may find a literature review useful in getting a feel for ethnographic research, perhaps in choosing a setting or a question for your

118   WRITING FROM VARIOUS DATA SOURCES

research or in understanding the issues of concern to those you will be observing in the field. In this case, use the guidelines for library research in Chapter 7 to get an overview of the sociological literature relevant to your project.

COLLECTING YOUR DATA

UNDERSTAND THE ASSIGNMENT

Where are you supposed to go? What are you to look for? Are you expected mainly to present your own reactions or to describe what others do in the setting? Is the task to demonstrate your ability to apply course concepts to what you see, to provide a detailed account of interaction in the observed settings, or both? Is there a specific question you should address?

PLAN AHEAD

1. Begin early in the quarter or semester. Field data cannot always be collected predictably or on short notice. Furthermore, you may have to return to your field setting several times to get the additional information or understanding that you need. Your time grid (see Chapter 2) can help you allot the time you will need.

2. Make arrangements to interview or observe. While the prospect of getting permission may make you anxious at first, you will find that most people are receptive to showing or telling you about their lives. You can assure them that their identities will remain confidential if the information is personal. Be sure to follow the procedures established by your college's Human Subjects and Ethics Committee, which might require you to submit your research plan for approval or to obtain written permission from those you observe or interview; consult your instructor for details.

When scheduling your observation or interview, allow plenty of time. Unanticipated events may occur, your subject may begin to talk at length about some particularly interesting topic, or you may think of additional questions on the spot. Also, you will need to allow time to record, transcribe, or elaborate on notes immediately after the contact.

3. Plan how you will record your data (a summary of recording options follows later in this chapter). In interview situations, it is best to tape-record or to make notes during the interview. Likewise, notes made while observing are more reliable than those made after you've left your field setting. The methods you choose will depend on the situation and your

personal style. But, whatever approach you take, be prepared ahead of time with adequate supplies of audiotape, batteries, paper, and pencils, as appropriate.

OBSERVE THE SETTING

Although you may know a lot about the setting and the interactions you observe, it is crucial that you leave behind your previous assumptions and even your knowledge about them in order to learn something new. Adopt the attitude of a naive outsider so that you can begin to look in a new way at events and experiences you used to take for granted. In other words, don't try to figure out beforehand what conclusions you should come to or how you will use the information you are collecting. Just be as attentive to detail as you can in order to get as much valuable information as possible.

When observing, don't presume you know which events or interactions matter most. Keep your eyes and ears open to everything that is going on around you. Notice your surroundings, all the people who are present, the time taken by events, and so on. Attempt, above all, to look at the setting or situation through the eyes of the participants.

When interviewing, follow these guidelines:

1. Don't talk more than you have to. Listen carefully to the respondent's comments.

2. Avoid leading questions that define the respondent's answer, and avoid questions that point to *yes* or *no* answers.

3. Rather than asking why something happened, concentrate on asking how it occurred. "Why" questions often put people on the defensive, making them feel forced to justify their actions or life-style. Also, respondents' answers to "how" questions are usually more specific about real events, providing you with the concrete examples you need to describe in detail what goes on in the setting.

4. Don't overwhelm your interviewee with multiple questions. If you are a new interviewer, you may be especially sensitive to silence, but don't rush in with comments, clarification, or further questions if the respondent pauses. Allow the respondent time to think and to complete his or her responses fully.

5. Encourage the respondent to be fairly specific about the details of events or experiences: Exactly who was involved? What happened? When did it take place? Remember, however, that probing should be gentle (for example, "Could you tell me more about that?"), not an interrogation.

6. Relax, allow your natural curiosity about your subject to direct you, and *listen*.

RECORD YOUR DATA

Since the final paper you produce will be only as good as your recorded data, it is crucial that you record observations or interview responses accurately, in detail, as soon as possible after the event. Otherwise, you will inevitably forget or distort what was said or done.

In observational research, take notes on what you see or hear as it happens. If that is impossible or bothers those you are observing, then record what you observed as soon as possible afterward. You may even want to take periodic note-taking breaks away from the setting during your observation to jot down a few words or phrases that will trigger your memory later.

If you are interviewing, it is best to tape-record the conversation (with the interviewee's permission). Don't be shy about asking permission to tape or take notes during the interview. People are often agreeable once they understand your interest in accurately representing what they say.

If subjects seem reluctant to let you tape, don't force the issue. Just listen to their responses and reconstruct the interview in writing as soon as you can afterward. Don't editorialize in your reporting of what was said. Likewise, don't edit your interview to make responses seem more sensible or because something seems "inconsequential." If you edit or editorialize, you may leave out something significant. Report all the respondent's comments, keeping them in their original order. And be sure to include all your questions, as well as the answers to them.

If you do tape-record an interview, it will be helpful to transcribe it into written form. There are special dictation machines that make transcription easier. Or, at the least, you should listen carefully to the interview and take notes on both your questions and the responses.

In all cases, make your notes specific. Describe in detail what you observed, did, and/or heard. Like a good reporter, give the specifics of who, what, when, and where. Include concrete details about the physical setting, what went on, and your reactions: How did you feel about the people with whom you were involved? Remember that in ethnographic field research, you are the research instrument; it is through your person, your interactions, and your relations that you learn about the people and settings you are studying. For that reason, your personal reactions are especially important.

You may be required to submit the originals, or a typed version, of your field notes as an appendix to your paper. Or you might choose to include your notes in an appendix, in order to give your instructor a better appreciation of what happened in your setting or interview (and of how hard you worked to gather your data!). Even if you will not be submitting your notes, keep them legible and organized. Be sure, for example, to date every entry. The quality of your paper relies on the quality of your field notes; the more clear data you have available, the stronger your paper will be.

EXAMPLE OF OBSERVATIONAL FIELD NOTES

The following sample observational field notes will give you an idea of their general format and content. The example is excerpted from the notes written up by a student in an introductory ethnography class. The assignment asked students to observe interactions in public settings. The student chose to observe a familiar scene that was part of her everyday life—riding the bus.

OUR COMMENTS

Unlike your final paper, which should be double-spaced, it is usually acceptable to single-space your field notes. However, be sure to leave wide margins, for comments (your own or the instructor's) and coding.

It's perfectly normal to be nervous about entering a new situation. Take a deep breath and try to relax. Like the subjects in these notes, many people being observed are quite friendly and very willing to talk about their work.

We all have assumptions about other people and the world we live in. What is challenging and fun about sociology is the opportunity to get past those assumptions and learn new ways of seeing things. Remember to keep an open mind.

Whenever possible, make a note right away of direct quotations. Otherwise, paraphrase as accurately as possible.

Notice how the drivers all keep looking at their watches! It's important to note as many little details as possible, even if you can't recall them all completely. This early observation about the bus driver's precision about time turned out to be a major theme in the field notes: through her observation, the author of these notes came to appreciate the rhythm of the bus driver's workday and the memory skill it takes to do the job.

Observation 3: Bus Riding

   With considerable trepidation, I boarded the bus to
campus with the intention of speaking to bus drivers about
their perceptions of bus riding and their role in it.
Previous observations had led me to the conclusion that bus
drivers were either identified with, or detached from, their
roles so much that their attitudes and behaviors were very
brusque and "macho." The first of many such assumptions was
shot down as I discovered that today's driver on my route
was a young Hispanic woman of slight build: hardly the burly
type at all! I approached her after everyone else had left
the bus at the campus terminal. I introduced myself, told
her that I would like to ask her a few questions about her
job for a class assignment. She said that she liked her job,
that "it's great if you like driving!" but that she had just
a few minutes. I asked her if I could wait at the terminal
for her after my class and ride the entire route with her.
She said sure, and explained a process I didn't completely
understand about how she would be replaced at 4th and
Colorado at 11-something that morning, for a lunch break,
but would be back on the route later, and her "last run of
the day" left UCLA at 3-something. I agreed I would wait on
campus until her later run passed through. What struck me
most was how precisely she knew the route and schedule:
"Fourth and Colorado" had such exactness, and sounded so
familiar to her; both times she mentioned about the schedule
were to the minute, and were from memory. As I stood to
leave, she glanced at her watch.
   I sat on the stairs which lead down to the bus terminal
after class that afternoon. I figured I might have a wait
of up to an hour and that I might as well try to work up
the nerve to talk to the drivers who hang around on the
stairs between runs, or who go up them to get a snack on
campus. One driver I was familiar with from riding his
route walked downstairs and commented that I had found a
"good seat, out of the sun." I told him that I was
observing bus riding. He said it [bus riding] is "very
interesting" and that I should "take a notebook or a tape

The question about how people "click off" on the bus is too directive. It doesn't produce much useful information. Contrast it to the more open-ended question that follows about what the *subject* thinks is the most outstanding feature about bus-riding.

Remember that your notes are not a formal treatise. Describe gesture, sounds, even smells, through whatever means necessary to bring the setting or conversation alive for your reader.

What did the subjects *do* that led the observer to believe they were preoccupied or hurried?

In many ways, you already have much practice at entering new social settings. Use your everyday conversational skills to make contact with your subject—they're "just people" too!

Notice how important the inclusion of the driver's "chuckle" is. Without noting it, it would be hard to tell whether he is being sarcastic or funny or what. Don't trust your memory to remind you. Even though it's obvious at the time, it's easy to forget when you observe many settings and talk to a number of people.

Notice the results of asking the subject what is outstanding (or interesting or unusual or important) about the setting *from his or her point of view.* An issue is raised that the observer had never considered, but that is central to the experience of bus driving. Much more information could have been elicited, however, by probing for details with "what" and "how" questions: *How* did the person try to get around paying the fare? *How* did the driver outsmart the two riders who wanted to avoid buying transfers? *What* excuses do people offer for not having the money?

recorder along on a ride." I asked if he'd ever noticed
something I'd observed, that people seem to "click off"
while on the bus, almost like they're not really there.
"Oh, sure, well some get sick on the bus, so they do other
things. That's why you hear the 'bzz-bzz' [the stop-the-bus
signal] so much. They suddenly [he mimes someone becoming
alert, looking around—indicating someone realizing where
they are]." He'd been pausing, moving slowly down the last
few steps; he now glanced at his watch, quickened his pace,
gestured in a wave, and returned to his bus.

There were a few other drivers coming and going, but I
didn't initiate any conversation. Some seemed hurried, some
preoccupied. One, however, was walking downstairs with a
snack. I commented that he'd gotten himself a treat. He said,
"I'm starving. I haven't had time to get something to eat." I
told him I was sorry I'd finished my banana already, or I'd
be happy to share it. We agreed on the ribsticking virtues of
bananas. [Food: the universal bond!] I told him I was
observing bus-riding for a class. He smiled. "That [bus-
riding] is really interesting. [Chuckle] Yep, that's really
interesting." I asked what feature he thought was most
outstanding about bus-riding. He said I should see the number
of ways people try to avoid paying. I indicated surprise,
since I'd never observed this. He assured me it was common,
and described a few instances—one person who tried to just
get out of paying the 85-cent fare, two guys who tried to
avoid having to buy transfers (and how he outsmarted them),
the ways people give excuses for not having the money.

EXAMPLE OF INTERVIEW NOTES

Following is a brief excerpt from the interview notes that Tiffany Seden (TS) took while researching her paper on the legal system for mental illness (see pp. 132–147). Although she could have asked for permission to make an audio recording of the interview, this example illustrates the type of notes jotted down during or immediately after speaking with her primary subject's psychiatrist, a medical doctor (DR).

TS: Why are you here today?

DR: Court needs to decide whether or not he is able to provide for self—adequate food, clothing, shelter. Whether or not he's a danger to self and others.

TS: What do you think he needs?

DR: Stay in treatment.

TS: What do you think of whole court process?

DR: Waste of time. Fifteen to twenty patients I have to see every day. Can't be wasting time here for eight hours/day. Second time I've had to be here this week.

The interview excerpt illustrates how Tiffany's bold move to speak directly to a participant in the process she observed paid off. The remarks she can attribute directly to the psychiatrist are very revealing about his perspective on the legal system related to mental illness. Being able to convey the voices of actual actors in a social scene makes her paper much richer and more graphic.

It is understandable and acceptable that Tiffany did not have time to take notes in complete sentences; the goal of her original notes was simply to make an accurate record of the conversation, which otherwise might be quickly distorted or forgotten. When using this excerpt in her paper, Tiffany just "fleshes out" her notes into the complete thoughts originally expressed in her interview. For example, the response she summarizes as "Stay in treatment" is returned to the original, "He needs to stay in treatment."

However, when she directly quotes these interview notes, as she does in her paper, Tiffany should *not* include material that wasn't actually noted at the time of the interview. For instance, her conclusion that the patient was more of a nuisance than a human being to this doctor could be included as part of the text of the paper, but it should not be cited as a direct quotation from her interview notes.

Two of Tiffany's inquiries are phrased as "what" questions, which typically elicit more useful information from interview subjects than "why" questions do. Also, her questions are open-ended. If she had asked, "Do you think the patient should be institutionalized?" the psychiatrist might have just responded "yes" or "no." Asking "What do you think . . . ?" allowed her subject to describe events in his own terms. She might have gotten more specific responses if she had been able to focus her questions. For example, "What do you think of this whole court process?" is a broad inquiry, to which the reply ("It's a waste of time") was very general. She might have learned even more if she had asked specifically what the subject thought of a particular aspect of the court process.

ORGANIZING YOUR DATA

The observations and answers you collect in your fieldwork are the data on which your paper will be based. In this step of your research process, you use the material you have collected to answer the question that your instructor assigned or that you formulated. This is an exciting process; as you look back over your notes, you will notice that the setting you have learned about in a personal way reveals interesting information about the nature of social life.

Answering an Assigned Question

If your instructor asked a specific question in your paper assignment, now is the time to consider how what you saw, heard, and experienced addresses that question. Here are some guidelines:

1. Go through your notes and make a mark by every comment, observation, or response that seems relevant to the question being asked. Don't be too discriminating at this point. Better to include too much at this stage than too little.

2. Copy these relevant pieces of data onto separate note cards, or photocopy your original notes and from the photocopy cut and paste the relevant excerpts onto the cards; this will allow you to lay the bits of data out side by side, much as you would for materials in a library research paper (see Chapter 7). Note that you should *never* cut up your original notes. Always save your originals and use photocopies or carbon copies for cutting. Also be sure to indicate on each card the page number of your field notes from which the excerpt was taken, so that you can include the citation if you quote the excerpt in your paper.

3. Now consider what the information on each card says in response to the question asked in the assignment. What does it tell you about the setting you observed and/or the people you interviewed?

4. Look for patterns among your cards. Move them around to illustrate to yourself how the information fits together. For instance, you might stack together cards that contain examples of the same kind of behavior. Or you might arrange appropriate cards to reflect stages in a process.

128   WRITING FROM VARIOUS DATA SOURCES

Course materials and the paper assignment itself may be useful in helping you notice the patterns in your data. Recall concepts covered in the class
that are relevant to your project. Review carefully just what the assignment
directs you to look at. Then consider how your data illustrate those concepts or teach you something about the social relations you observed.

For instance, Tiffany Seden, the student author of the sample ethnographic paper that appears at the end of this chapter, was asked by her
instructor to observe and write about social responses to troublesome behavior. The instructor recommended two articles that would be useful to
students in considering what they observed in the court setting Tiffany
chose. These readings contained judges' strategies for determining
whether to release or recommit psychiatric patients petitioning to leave
the hospital. In analyzing her observation and interview notes, Tiffany
might have listed these strategies, and then stacked in separate piles excerpts from her data that illustrated them. In fact, you will note in her
paper that she uses subheadings ("Ability to Provide Necessities," "Caretaker," "Commitment to Further Treatment") to highlight her observations
of each strategy. In this way, she is able to draw a clear link between her
observations and the relevant course materials.

Answering a Broader Question

Perhaps you were simply assigned (or chose as your project) to participate in and describe a social setting. It will still be useful to sort out excerpts from your notes as described in the preceding section, but you will
probably have more freedom to establish the categories into which you
will organize your observations.

Begin by carefully rereading your field notes to refresh your memory
about the events. Then start to look for patterns in your notes. As in the
case of an assigned question, you might use course concepts to organize
this search. Better yet, you might try to find the categories and terms used
by people you observed, asking yourself how *they* understand and describe
their activities.

For example, if you were taking a course in deviant behavior, your text
would probably spend considerable space defining "deviance" in terms of
breaking social norms. But in ethnographic research, you would find that
the people you observe don't talk about "deviance" or "norms." Thus,
rather than looking in your notes for examples of what your text would
define as "deviance," it would be more enlightening to pinpoint what specific behaviors your subjects perceive as odd or disruptive and to note the
ways in which they categorize and describe those who exhibit disliked behavior (such as referring to them as "weird" or as "different from us").
Similarly, a course in stratification may present sophisticated ways of
measuring socioeconomic status; but, since the most interesting and valuable findings from your ethnographic field research concern the ways in

which the people you observe perceive their own position in relation to society, you might look through your notes for all the ways they compare themselves to other groups.

Some of the most common themes ethnographers look for include the ways members characterize their group; the ways they distinguish between insiders and outsiders; the special language they develop to describe their shared activities and values; their patterns of interaction; the ways they teach new members the ropes; the ways they identify and respond to behavior they don't like; and the ways in which members experience their setting through the course of an event, a workday, or any other unit of experience. You may find some or all of these reflected in your notes and you may find interesting themes not listed here. You may choose to focus on one area or on several related themes.

As you begin to identify themes that run through your field notes, you can proceed to sort the excerpts into piles, as described in the preceding section.

WRITING YOUR PAPER

Because ethnographic field research does not involve hypothesis-testing, the essay format discussed in Chapter 1 is more appropriate than the journal format for this type of paper. Simply modify it slightly: in place of the three (or more) "claims" or "points" relevant to a paper that proposes and supports a thesis, substitute the themes or concepts that you identified in your field notes. These will serve as the body of your paper. Even though an ethnography does not always propose an answer and attempt to prove why it is more "accurate," remember that you are responsible for demonstrating, through effective use of your data, why your description of the setting is believable. Be sure to describe your research methods—where you went, how long you stayed, with whom you spoke, and so on—and to include as evidence the most illustrative excerpts from your field notes.

If the question you are addressing was assigned, you can use one of two approaches to present a written report on your observations:

First, you can describe what happened or what was said, chronologically, and comment on how course concepts apply to the things you describe, as you report them in the order in which they occurred. This is the strategy employed in the sample paper in this chapter.

Second, you can organize your paper around concepts, defining and indicating the importance of each, and using your data to illustrate them. In this case, you can follow the essay format, taking for each of your main points a selected concept or group of concepts.

Unless your assignment specifically requires one approach, either can be successful. If you are uncertain about which approach to take, or which may be preferred, discuss your plans with your instructor. In either case, return to course concepts and themes frequently. Ask yourself how the events or comments you are describing reflect or illustrate sociological ideas. This will help you avoid the common mistake of making overly psychological interpretations of those whom you observe or interview.

If your assignment doesn't specify a particular question for you to answer or a specific setting for you to analyze according to course concepts, then you can simply organize the themes you discovered in your notes into the essay format. You might choose three points to make about one of the themes that you found most interesting or revealing. Or, you might develop your paper around three different themes.

Whichever format you use, it is important for your paper to incorporate the reactions you experienced in your research and recorded in your notes. Inevitably, those engaged in ethnographic field research encounter people, events, and experiences that fascinate, surprise, confuse, or even upset them. It is a challenge to make effective use of such reactions without getting sidetracked into self-analysis. A good way to make your personal reactions relevant is to ask yourself what they illuminate about the setting. Describe in your paper how your own feelings and thoughts helped you better understand the people you studied and their interactions.

When writing your paper, you may quote your field notes directly. When you do, punctuate and cite them as you would any other source. Or, you may choose to summarize an incident or a response in an anecdotal way to illustrate a point. As long as they are relevant to your assignment, use your collected data in as many ways as you can; they make up the empirical basis for your discussion.

SUGGESTED READINGS

Emerson, Robert M. 1983. *Contemporary Field Research: A Collection of Readings.* Boston: Little, Brown.
Emerson, Robert M., Rachel I. Fretz, and Linda L. Shaw. 1995. *Writing Fieldnotes.* Chicago: University of Chicago Press.
Van Maanen, John. 1988. *Tales of the Field: On Writing Ethnography.* Chicago: University of Chicago Press.

A SAMPLE STUDENT PAPER

The following sample ethnographic field research paper was written by Tiffany Seden for a class in the sociology of mental illness. Choosing between two options the instructor offered for observing and writing about social responses to troublesome behavior, Tiffany visited Court 95, where writs of *habeas corpus* are brought by patients seeking release from a psychiatric hospital. Judges must gather information about each case and decide whether the patient should be hospitalized involuntarily or released from the institution. Tiffany observed and spoke to participants in one case before, during, and after its hearing.

Tiffany's title, along with her introductory remarks, highlight the idea she used as the theme for her paper: that the decision whether or not to commit an individual for involuntary psychiatric hospitalization depends less on the person's sad, mad, or odd behavior than on the social circumstances in which he or she lives. Tiffany uses her original data to illustrate this point, which is made in several assigned readings for the course. Notice how she consistently makes connections between concepts drawn from these course readings and the empirical data she collected. Her conclusions are supported with specific observations, which she summarized in her field notes. Many of our comments relate to her use of her observational notes: although she has elaborated on her observations in a way that makes them very dramatic and interesting, such elaborations should be included directly in the text of her paper; only her original notes should be quoted directly.

Tiffany's paper demonstrates that she is a capable and diligent student. She has succeeded in grasping several complex concepts regarding the sociology of mental illness. She is a good example of a student whose good writing could be made even better by applying a closer eye to such details as grammar and punctuation.

Finally, Tiffany's paper reflects her sociological imagination by connecting the experiences of one person—Michael, a psychiatric patient she spoke to while observing in Court 95—with broad social processes, such as the social control of disruptive behavior.

OUR COMMENTS

Because of the length of Tiffany's paper, she has included a title page (as recommended in Chapter 5).

The Legal System for Mental Illness:
Cure or Containment?

Tiffany Seden
Sociology 148
Professor Pollner
December 9, 1991

Tiffany's first paragraph introduces the reader to the course perspectives and concepts relevant to her paper. In it, she cites the sources of both *specific terms* (Goffman's "organizational havoc") and *ideas* (Horwitz's notion of "mental illness" as a label) she is using.

Tiffany should include a description of the methods she used to gather the data for this paper: readers need to know how she got her information, in order to assess the conclusions she draws from it. Some readers would benefit from a brief description of the assignment as well as some background information on California's commitment procedures.

In place of her fourth sentence, a stronger, more direct statement of Tiffany's learning process would be: "After reading Holstein's "The Placement of Insanity" and visiting Court 95, I concluded that. . . ."

Tiffany does a good job of using her field notes to illustrate her point. Her notes successfully capture the scene she observed, and the patient's place in it. *However, the format of the notes she uses throughout this paper poses a significant problem:* it's not clear whether descriptions such as these are taken directly from her notes (if so, the source should be cited) or are her elaborations of them (if so, they should be included directly in the text). Remember that quoted notes should be presented as close as possible to their original form. The citation should be put at the end of the quotation and be formatted like this example: "You know, I fight off demons too. That's why I took the name Michael" (Seden 1991). Finally, she should make it clear that she has created a pseudonym to protect the anonymity of her research subject.

When observers find an individual's behavior incomprehensible they are likely to apply labels of mental illness (Horwitz 1982, p. 16). When these behaviors disrupt community life, a conflict over claims of place arises and thus exposes that order to what Goffman calls "organizational havoc" (Holstein 1984, p. 35). Through the use of legal proceedings, judges may inflict involuntary mental hospitalization upon those who they deem possess a "grave disability." However, my visit to Court 95 and reading Holstein's "The Placement of Insanity" helped lead me to the conclusion that a "grave disability" is not taken as sufficient reason to hospitalize an individual against his or her will. A more important criterion is the "viability" of the individual's living situation and the capacity for that situation to control the havoc related to their mental illness. I was also awakened to the notion that the goal of hospitalization "is not to cure the patient but to contain him in a niche in free society where he can be tolerated" (Goffman 1981, p. 180). Thus, the regard for the patient's cure is minimal and the concern for a more "havoc-free" environment is of utmost importance.

In order to maintain this "havoc-free" environment, judges may sentence "gravely disabled" individuals to involuntary hospitalization. Grave disability associated with mental disorder means that an individual is self-endangering or socially disturbing.

The following case, observed both in the waiting room and inside Court 95, describes a "gravely disabled" individual:

> Patrick John Michael Reilly, a 32-year-old white male, was a manic depressive with signs of euphoria, irritability, delusions, and little sleep.
> "My name is Patrick John Michael Reilly. My Catholic name is Michael, after St. Michael who fought off demons. You know, I fight off demons too. That's why I took the name Michael. Did you get that?"
> His posture was perfect. His eyes were wide. His hands tightly gripped the seat of the chair almost lifting himself up. The court guards entered the waiting room where Patrick and I were talking. "Sing the Thorazine song." Patrick began to sing loudly,

Tiffany might bolster her credibility by including attribution to authors directly in the text, such as "However, *according to Holstein,* judges expect . . ." and "Also, *Goffman maintains that* hospitalization is considered to be a last resort. . . ."

Be sure to doublecheck for punctuation (such as using an apostrophe to show the possessive of "psychiatrist") and usage and spelling (the singular form of "diagnoses," needed here, is "diagnosis").

Tiffany does not make the source of this list clear. Her format—indented and single-spaced—implies that she is quoting, but no source is cited.

Caution! Verbs must always match their subjects. In the first sentence following the list of criteria, the subject "any" is singular. Therefore, Tiffany's predicate should be *"is* not present." Likewise, pronouns must match the nouns they refer to: the sentence should read, "a person's [singular] inability to care for *him-* or *herself,"* rather than "for themselves [plural]."

disrupting the entire T.V. room. "He's really fucked
up," added the other guard who was constantly taunting
and encouraging Patrick's extreme behavior.
     Frequently Patrick became socially disruptive and
harmful to himself and others. We can see this in his
physician's testimony:
     "On the eleventh he was brought into the emergency
room by his three-hundred-pound roommate and a social
worker. His mood was euphoric and irritable. He was
singing and screaming in front of his board and care.
He was hyperverbal and joking. He put a hole in the
wall of the nursing station."

It is evident from Patrick's fabrications and actions that
he is indeed mentally ill. However, judges expect that most
of the individuals brought before the court are in fact
extremely disturbed (Holstein 1984, p. 40). Also,
hospitalization is considered to be a last resort when
other options of care are nonexistent: "There has been some
pressure to keep the potential patient in the community as
long as possible . . ." (Goffman 1981, p. 180). The laws in
California coincide with this theory so closely that
involuntary commitment is difficult to arrange. Thus, even
though judges may believe the patient is severely mentally
ill, the symptoms of mental illness and a psychiatrists
diagnoses is not enough to distinguish between those who
will be hospitalized and those who will be set free. Judges
use the following criteria to decide whether or not to
subject an individual to involuntary commitment:

1. The person's ability to provide life's basic
   necessities.
2. The willing presence of a "caretaker" to supervise the
   candidate patient.
3. The candidate patient's cooperation with a community-
   based treatment/custody regime.

If any of these three elements are not present, disruption
is unavoidable, and hospitalization becomes more likely
(Holstein 1984, p. 35). Therefore, "grave disability" does

Here again, it is important to watch out for inconsistency between nouns and the possessive pronouns related to them. Tiffany may be seeking to use nonsexist language by using a collective pronoun ("themself") rather than a limiting singular male one ("himself"); if so, she must be sure to precede it with a plural noun ("However disabled *patients* may be, the ability to provide *themselves . . .*").

Tiffany has located a good excerpt from her field notes to illustrate the points she read about in Holstein's article. However, her presentation would be smoother with a transition, such as "The following observation illustrates the line of questioning Holstein describes."

Tiffany uses her field notes to bring her reader into the courtroom with her. However, it does not seem from this example that she has used an excerpt from her original notes, which would be most effective, but has included a later description and elaboration of her observations.

not merely entail a person's inability to care for
themselves. A tenable living environment with the ability
to maintain peaceful surroundings is even more substantial.
Under these circumstances, in order for Patrick to be
committed under California law, he must also lack one of
the above three criteria.

Ability to Provide Necessities
However disabled a patient may be, the ability to
provide themselves with life's basic necessities is primary.
Holstein's article lists a few questions the judge may ask:
"Does the person eat regularly? Can the person shop for and
prepare food? Does the person dress him- or herself? Does
the person have a place to stay?" (Holstein 1984, p. 45).

> The judge asked Patrick's physician, "Is he disabled?"
> Dr. Powers took a deep breath and pushed his lips
> together and let out his breath while tilting his head
> to the side, which showed boredom, and responded,
> "Yes." The judge, wanting more of a response, asked him
> for more information. "Why do you think he cannot
> provide himself with food, clothing, or shelter?" The
> doctor looked up at the ceiling, tilting his head
> slightly and bringing his head back down he looked back
> at the floor. "His irritability prevents a
> manageability. He's not stable enough to be discharged.
> He refused his medications; however, he has been taking
> them since Tuesday because of the hearing."

Judges are also concerned about a patient's income. A
patient dependent upon assistance payments such as Social
Security, Social Security Insurance, Social Security
Disability Insurance, and unemployment, is more financially
secure than those who live a more independent life by
working and renting a private apartment (Holstein 1984, p.
16). The reasoning behind this is that the mentally ill
have a more difficult time holding onto a job, so financial
stability is not assured when they are supporting
themselves.

For consistency with "patient's," the pronoun that follows it should be singular *("himself"* or *"herself").*

When Tiffany writes, "Because the patient is mentally ill . . . ," she is veering away from the sociological perspective presented by the course materials serving as the foundation for her paper. The sociological stance used by Holstein and Horwitz, for example, emphasizes that mental illness is a label applied to only *some* people displaying disturbed or disruptive behavior.

Tiffany does a good job here of recognizing the relationship between ideas presented in course readings and what she observed in the field.

Tiffany's recurrent trouble with pronouns strikes again. (The plural pronoun *"their"* incorrectly follows a singular subject *"the patient."*) This is a common example of a good writer whose work could be made even stronger with some fine-tuning.

Without an overview of the legal process being observed, this reference to a "prosecuting attorney" is confusing to the reader.

> The judge asked Patrick's physician whether or not
> Patrick had an income. Dr. Powers answered, "Yes," in
> a low voice, looking straight at the floor just in
> front of the witness stand. The judge asked, "SS, SSI,
> SSDI, and unemployment?" In the same monotone voice,
> still looking at the floor, Dr. Powers answered,
> "Yes."

This exchange illustrates that the patient's mental status
is not primary, and the judge's concern may lie with the
practical circumstances of the patient's ability to provide
themselves with the basic necessities.

Caretaker

Because the patient is mentally ill, everyday tasks
become problematic. Thus, a judge may prefer that someone
live near the patient for supervision. Holstein states that
"Caretakers are seen as necessary components of a tenable
living situation for a person who is seriously mentally
ill" (Holstein 1984, p. 51). According to Holstein, "family
members, the staff of board and care homes, physicians,
landlords, neighbors and the staff at the Salvation Army or
the local rescue mission may serve as acceptable
caretakers" (Holstein 1984, p. 53). This caretaker must be
competent and enforce medication and treatment. Patrick's
board and care served as a sufficient caretaker.

Commitment to Further Treatment

The judge also elicits the cooperation of the patient to
commit to a treatment for their disturbances. Because
Patrick lived in a board and care facility, supervision is
not as good as supervision by a parent or spouse, and
therefore, before the judge released him, she made sure that
Patrick would continue taking his medication on his own:

> "Would you like to stay in the board and care?" asked
> the prosecuting attorney. "Yes," Patrick answered,
> trying to contain himself, taking short breaths, "I
> came to the hospital having seizures." Patrick went
> into great detail describing his seizure. "If the

The possessive form requires an apostrophe: *"judge's."*

Note how Tiffany uses her field notes as evidence, just as she might refer to materials from a book, article, or lecture. They should be cited, just as other materials would be.

Tiffany's sociological perspective is slipping here. She refers to "mental illness" as a disease—as something to be "cured," with "symptoms" to be controlled. This differs from the view of it as a label, which Holstein and Goffman adopt.

Here is a different kind of subject/pronoun confusion. It's not clear what noun the pronoun "their" refers to. Is it the *"judges"* who have a "need for containment"? Similarly, who has an illness that needs a cure?

This indented quotation, part of Tiffany's conversation with the patient's psychiatrist, is discussed at length in the previous section, "Example of Interview Notes." Note here, however, that the indented material—which should be reserved for direct quotation of field notes—inappropriately includes Tiffany's later conclusions.

doctor prescribes medication will you take it?" "Yes,"
Patrick raises his voice and becomes angry. "Yes, only
if he prescribes only those four medications."

The judges main concern was that Patrick take his
prescribed psychotropic medication. She never asked if he
would continue seeing his doctor for psychotherapy. He even
told the judge in his final statements that he didn't like
his doctor:

> "You may step down now if you've said everything you
> want to say," said the judge. Patrick takes on a
> tough-guy tone: "I want a new doctor. . . ."

Medication does not cure the mentally ill; it merely
controls the symptoms. Nonetheless, Patrick's release was
partly determined by whether or not he would resume taking
his medication rather than by his commitment to
psychotherapeutic treatment. Thus, the preservation of a
havoc-free environment was a greater priority than was
Patrick's cure.

Judges based their decision regarding involuntary
commitment on criteria related to their need for
containment, rather than on finding a cure for their
illness. My conversations with others in the court process
revealed a similar lack of concern with helping the
patient. In talking to Patrick's physician, I realized that
Patrick was just a job to him:

> "Why are you here today?" I asked the doctor, who
> seemed very irritated. "The court needs to decide
> whether or not he is able to provide for himself
> adequate food, clothing, and shelter. Whether or not
> he's a danger to himself and others," the doctor took
> a deep breath of boredom. "What do you think he
> needs?" I asked. "He needs to stay in treatment," he
> answered. "What do you think of this whole court
> process?" "It's a waste of time. I have fifteen to

Tiffany's reference to the "norms that we take for granted" is a good *sociological* description of the patient's problems. However, her references to "his illness" and "problems that most of us solve subconsciously" are more psychological than is appropriate for the course.

Tiffany uses her conclusion to express some of her opinions about what she observed in the field. Note, however, that she keeps expression of her personal feelings brief. The strength of her paper is that it is based on the empirical data she collected and analyzed.

twenty patients I have to see every day. I can't be
wasting my time here for eight hours a day. This is
the second time I've had to be here this week." I
felt like he really didn't care what happened to
Patrick. Patrick was more of a nuisance than a human
being.

The guards also didn't show much care or consideration for
the patients:

"Sing the Thorazine song." "Do your Elvis impression."
"This guy has a really sick background." The guards
would laugh at and taunt Patrick. I knew it bothered
him because of the way he responded: "When people make
fun of me I need to walk or do push-ups." Then he
knelt down and did fifty push-ups.

These conversations and observations lead to the conclusion
that concern for the patient as a person is minimal.

After I left Court 95, I thought about the four hours
that I had spent with Patrick and a few things stuck out in
my mind. I was there just a little while, and Patrick has
to live with himself and his illness all the time. He has
difficulty thinking out problems that most of us solve
subconsciously. The norms that we take for granted—like
staying calm and composed in a waiting room—are obstacles
for Patrick.

Finally, I realized that the legal system isn't designed
to look for cures. However, these patients are people, too.
They are sensitive to those who make fun of them. This
ridicule by the court guards and uncaring treatment from
doctors does not help the patient's predicament. No one
seems to really care about the possibility of a cure and
are more concerned with laughing at people who are
different or simply with putting them where they can't
bother anyone. My observations in Court 95 led me to
believe that the court system needs to pay closer attention
to the patient's needs and less to getting the job over
with.

References should be put on a separate page, as Tiffany has done.

Tiffany should have included her interview and/or field notes in her list of references. Since the format was not specified in the assignment, she should have discussed the required information and preferred format with her instructor. Here is one possibility:

Seden, Tiffany. November 25, 1991. Field notes, observation of Court 95, Superior Court, Los Angeles, CA.

REFERENCES

Goffman, Erving. [1969] 1981. "The Insanity of Place." Pp.
    179-201 in *The Sociology of Mental Illness*, edited by O.
    Grusky and M. Pollner. New York: Holt, Rinehart, and
    Winston.
Holstein, James A. 1984. "The Placement of Insanity." *Urban*
    Life 14: 35-62.
Horwitz, Allan V. 1982. *The Social Control of Mental*
    Illness. Orlando: Academic Press.

9

THE QUANTITATIVE
RESEARCH PAPER

In a quantitative paper, numerical data are collected to answer a sociological question. Because quantitative research depends on specific techniques of data collection and analysis, this chapter (unlike the previous
three chapters) may be most useful to students who have taken or are taking an introductory research methods course.

Most quantitative papers are based on deductive reasoning—that is, the
investigator, starting with a theory or with previous research, expects a
certain answer to her or his research question. The investigator develops
one or more hypotheses with the aim of predicting the results. However,
some quantitative papers are based on inductive reasoning. The investigator, unsure of the answer but with some idea of what to look for, sets
out to explore a particular topic. Here the purpose is description rather
than prediction. No matter which approach is taken, the data collected
can be represented numerically.

The sample quantitative research paper that appears at the end of this
chapter illustrates both types of logic. The student writer, Alvin Hasegawa,
uses the deductive approach in examining the relationship between student
dating patterns and the prestige ranking of the student's fraternity or sorority. But he uses the inductive approach in examining the differential ranking of five date characteristics by high- and low-status "Greeks." Basing his
expectation on theory and previous research, Alvin anticipated that prestige ranking would be related to dating patterns. However, his theory did
not suggest anything specific about whether high- or low-prestige students
would rate date characteristics in any particular way. Therefore, he was not
sure how each of the two groups would rate the five date characteristics.

Like most quantitative research papers, Alvin's is written in journal
rather than essay format (see the section in Chapter 1, Developing an Ar-

gument: Logic and Structure, for more information on these two formats). In addition, the quantitative research paper is divided into the following four major sections. You should insert an extra line or two of space between sections. Capitalize and center the heading that labels each section (except for the introduction, which needs no heading). The issues that should be covered in each section include:

1. **Introduction:** After a review of the relevant theory and literature, what sociological question do you feel needs to be addressed? What, if any, expectations (hypotheses) do you have about the answer?
2. **Methods:** What method did you use in trying to answer your question? How did you select your sample? What measures did you use? What procedures did you follow?
3. **Results:** What patterns of numerical data did you find?
4. **Discussion:** What do your data mean? How do they relate to theory and/or previous research? Do the data support or refute your hypotheses?

Although the length of these four sections is generally about equal for published papers utilizing sophisticated methods and analyses, the introduction and discussion sections for student papers are generally slightly longer than the other two sections. However, the relative length of the sections will depend on the amount of detail required by your instructor for describing your methods and results. In addition to these four major sections, other important components of your paper include the title, abstract, references, and appendix (which are discussed later in the chapter).

Since journal styles vary, ask your instructor which professional or scholarly journal you should use as a guide. Before starting your paper, examine recent articles from the recommended journal. (If none is recommended, use the *American Sociological Review*.) Photocopy, or carefully read through, one or two sample journal articles to use as a model of format and tone. Your paper should not only look professional but sound professional as well. Scientific communication uses a formal prose style.

Collecting and analyzing quantitative data can be time-consuming tasks. Unanticipated problems or events may interfere. Start early in the term and apportion enough time on your time grid (see Chapter 2) for these and other tasks.

We have arranged the topics covered in this chapter according to the steps you should follow in writing your quantitative research paper. For example, although the title and the abstract go at the beginning of your paper, you should write them during the final stages so that they describe your entire study. Therefore, we cover these components toward the end of the chapter.

WRITING THE INTRODUCTION

The first step in preparing a quantitative paper is to write the introduction, even before collecting your data or selecting your method. The introduction guides your research and helps determine your focus, which is what Alvin Hasegawa discovered. When we asked him about his paper he told us: "When I write I like to start with the introduction, to work from the beginning to end. That is different than many people who start with the body [methods section] of the paper. . . . I try to make the introduction creative and interesting. Once I get the introduction down, the body of the paper flows well."

The purpose of the introduction is to provide a context for the formulation and operationalization of your hypotheses. Writing the introduction involves searching and reviewing the literature, stating the problem and framing a sociological question, and, where appropriate, developing hypotheses.

REVIEWING THE LITERATURE

Once you decide on a topic, use the reference sources listed in Chapter 7 (such as *Sociological Abstracts* and the *Social Science Citation Index*) to search for similar empirical studies of the topic. Also gather books and articles on the theory you plan to use as a framework for your study. Read and take notes as you would for a library research paper.

In writing your review of the literature, provide enough background material to place the hypotheses in their proper setting. Begin your review with a summary of the theory (or theories) from which your question is derived, specifying its major tenets and focusing on one or two aspects (or major concepts) that you would like to test. Next, discuss each relevant study, summarizing in a few sentences the theoretical approach, major hypotheses, operational definitions (measures), and conclusions drawn in each one. It is often helpful to arrange the studies in chronological order. How do these studies fit together? Do they form a pattern or are they inconsistent? Do they fail to account for an important variable? What direction do they suggest for future research?

STATING THE PROBLEM AND CHOOSING A QUESTION

The statement of the problem reveals the gaps or contradictory findings that you found after reviewing the chosen theory and relevant literature. Its purpose is to point out theoretical inconsistencies in need of resolution, methodological problems apparent in the empirical literature, and/or the logical next step that research in this area should take. For example, you may want to concentrate on a different interpretation of a theory not adequately tested; set up a critical test of two rival theories; extend the theory to a new population or substantive area; use a new operational definition of a concept; correct the faulty methodology of a previous study; use a different design or method; or include more variables in order to look for possible interactions. For some class assignments a simple replication of a published study may be sufficient. Be sure to check with your instructor. However, unless your study is an exact replication of an earlier study, you must explain how your study differs from previous works, how your study will extend their findings, and what your study will contribute.

Following from the review of the literature, the statement of the problem should suggest questions that need to be answered (for example, "Is education always related to occupational attainment?"). These questions can be refined and developed into hypotheses (for example, "If ethnicity is held constant, an increase in education will be associated with an increase in occupational attainment"). Most quantitative papers examine more than one hypothesis.

Stating Your Hypotheses

A hypothesis in a quantitative paper is the counterpart of the thesis in a library research paper. Each is a formal statement expressing the relationship you expect to find between two or more of your variables. Your literature review and statement of the problem show the logic that led to the development of your hypotheses. They serve as a sort of preliminary evidence. If your reasoning is sound, the numerical data you collect will provide further support for each of your hypotheses.

Each hypothesis should be stated in such a way that it can be unambiguously confirmed or rejected by the results. Each should also be stated in such a way as to make clear the type (causal or correlational) and direction (positive or negative) of the expected relationships. That is, does any particular hypothesis postulate that one variable causes the other, or does it simply state that the two variables are correlated? If the relationship is believed to be correlational rather than causal, are the variables expected to be related positively (as X increases, Y increases) or negatively (as X increases, Y decreases)? Explain how the independent and dependent variables will be operationally defined; that is, the manner in which the variables will be measured. For example, occupational attainment may be operationally defined as whether the job involves the supervision of other workers. (In correlational studies where there is no assumption about the causal order of the variables, no distinction is made between the independent and dependent variables.) Be sure to specify your unit of analysis; for example, individuals, groups, institutions, or countries.

As we explained earlier, if your study is purely exploratory you will not have specific hypotheses. You may simply have questions that suggest themselves as interesting problems in need of further investigation. In this case, you should explain why you feel an exploration of these topics is important. For some topics, a descriptive study is often an important first step toward the formulation of a good deductive study.

DEVELOPING A METHODS
AND ANALYSIS PLAN

Once you have drafted the introduction (except for the operational definitions of your variables), you are ready to proceed with the development of a methods and analysis plan. (Later, after you have completed the rest of your paper, you will revise and polish your introduction.) Conducting a sound investigation is crucial to writing a good quantitative research paper. Therefore, it is necessary to consider in advance all the decisions you must make in collecting your data. Drawing up a methods and analysis plan will greatly improve the quality of your paper and will make the writing process go more smoothly. Although it is beyond the scope of this book to discuss the multitude of methodological and statistical factors that need to be considered in conducting a good quantitative study, we do address those issues important to writing a good report of your study. These tips should be useful to both the novice and the more experienced student. However, if you are currently taking a research methods or statistics course, or have taken one or both in the past, you might want to consult your text(s) for further details.

You will be limited to certain methods depending on the kind of question you are trying to answer. For example, if you are interested in the mortality (death) rates of upper- versus lower-class men, you obviously would have to use archival sources rather than a survey. Your choice of method will also be influenced by your assignment and time and cost constraints. However, the four most common methods are archival sources, structured field observation, experiment, and survey.

Archival sources are records of preexisting data. Although some of these data are obtained from surveys—the Census, for example—we include them as archival because the results are published in tables available in government documents and books. Most of these data consist of official records of "rates," such as birth, death, marriage, divorce, crime, suicide, and accident rates. For example, you may want to examine the change in divorce rates from 1950 to 1984, the crime rates in urban versus rural areas, or the suicide rates of males versus females. For statistics about the United States, two excellent government publications are the annual *Statistical Abstract of the United States* and the *Historical Statistics of the United States: Colonial Times to 1970* (1989), both of which are available in most college and university libraries.

Structured field observation, unlike ethnographic field research, is guided by set hypotheses or specific measurement objectives. Structured observation can often involve simple counting, such as counting the occurrence of certain behaviors or the number of people in different situations. For instance, you may want to observe the frequency with which men as compared to women make supportive statements during group discussions, or count the number of students who use the coffeehouse for studying at different times during the day.

There are many different *experimental* designs, but the basic model involves two groups—an experimental group and a control group. Both groups are treated exactly the same except for the independent variable(s), which is manipulated. Although we usually think of experiments as conducted in a laboratory, experiments can also be conducted in everyday settings (called "field experiments"). For example, you may want to examine whether people in a shopping mall are more likely to come to the aid of a well-dressed victim or a shabbily dressed victim. You could manipulate the situation so that in half the cases your confederate (accomplice) comes to the mall wearing a suit, and in the other half wearing dirty jeans and a torn T-shirt.

The *survey* method includes both questionnaires and interviews. The logic of the survey is to replicate the experimental method artificially, although without the same degree of control, by comparing two or more groups. The groups can be based on response scores (for example, those who score high or low on a particular attitude measure) or on demographic characteristics (for example, Catholics and Protestants, blacks and whites, young and old, high and low socioeconomic status). If you are interested in the different responses of males and females to a series of questions, your independent variable would be sex of respondent. In a survey, unlike an experiment, the independent variable is not manipulated. Instead, the researcher focuses on response differences that result from the naturally existing differences in the respondents.

Whichever method you choose, be sure that your proposed research is in line with the guidelines set forth by the Human Subjects and Ethics Committee on your campus (ask your instructor for details). You may need to get approval for your project from this committee.

Once you have decided on a method, draw up a plan for data collection and analysis to show your instructor. A methods and analysis plan ensures, *before you collect the data,* that your study will actually provide a test of your hypotheses. Further, it guarantees that you will be able to make sense of your data and analyze them successfully. Many students waste time and effort collecting large amounts of data only to discover later that the data do not provide a test of their hypotheses. Or, they find that they don't know how to go about analyzing the data. A methods and analysis plan can prevent these problems.

When you write your methods and analysis plan, address those issues relevant to your type of study:

1. **What population will you sample?** How will you select your sample? If you are conducting a structured field study, what setting did you

choose? Do you anticipate any problems in gaining access to the respondents or the field setting? How many respondents (of each type) do you need to question? How many observations do you need to make?

2. **What measures will you use?** That is, how will you operationalize your variables? How long will the questionnaire or survey take to answer? If you plan on conducting an interview or survey, will you use closed-ended questions (also known as "fixed-response") or open-ended questions? Closed-ended questions compare to open-ended questions as multiple-choice exams compare to short-answer essay exams. What will be the possible range of the response scale (for example, a five-point Likert response scale) for the closed-ended questions?

If you plan to do a structured field observation, what exactly will you look for? How long should each observation last? What things will you want to have on your observation checklist (the list of things that you intend to count or measure)? For example, if you want to observe differences in how near people of different cultures stand to one another, you might want to have a checklist that includes several different ethnicities and distances.

If you will conduct an archival study, you will need to go to the library to find out the types of data that are available to you. Further, you will need to determine the form in which these data are presented. For example, if you are interested in comparing the birthrates of different religious groups, you will need to find out if the birthrates presented in the Census tables are broken down by religious affiliation. Librarians can very often help you find what you need.

If you plan to conduct an interview or survey, you will need to develop a questionnaire. Even when conducting an experiment in the laboratory or in the field, you generally will want to interview respondents or have them complete a questionnaire at the conclusion of the experiment. Although it is beyond the scope of this book to discuss all the details of creating a sound instrument, there are general guidelines that you should consider in order to facilitate the writing of your report. Instructors often expect you to include a copy of your instrument in the appendix of your paper. It is best to include your instrument in your methods and analysis plan and to have it approved by your instructor before you collect your data.

In developing your measures, it is best to begin by looking at those developed by other researchers. Scales exist that have already been shown to be valid and reliable. Many of these scales are reproduced in the appendixes of books or journal articles; others appear in *Measures of Social Psychological Attitudes* by John Robinson and Philip Shaver of the Survey Research Center at the University of Michigan's Institute for Survey Research. If you use an existing scale, be sure to refer to the name of the scale and its originator in the body of your paper (for example, "Rotter's Locus of Control Scale was administered to respondents") and to include the source of the scale in your list of references.

However, you might want to construct some original questions to use in conjunction with an existing scale or to modify existing questions to better suit the purpose of your study. In constructing your own questions, try to avoid the following pitfalls:

- Avoid using ambiguous terms or slang. Define the terms you use. For example, in Alvin's questionnaire, he defines what he means by the term "date" (see Table 9-1). Since dating patterns have changed over the years, there may have been some confusion as to what he meant by this term had he not clarified this point. (Although Alvin's questionnaire should appear on a separate page at the end of his paper, we've reproduced it here as an illustration.)
- Avoid "double-barreled" questions. Questions that contain "and" or "or" (such as "Do you feel that physical attractiveness or attitude similarity are important characteristics in a dating partner?") make it impossible to know whether the respondent views one or both characteristics as important. The way Alvin presents his questions eliminates this problem.
- Avoid biased questions that lead the respondent to answer in a socially desirable way. For example, rather than asking, "Have you ever had a date?" Alvin asks the question, "Have you dated in the last year?" Respondents may be reluctant to say that they have never dated. However, they may feel comfortable saying they have not dated recently.

With regard to other aspects of your instrument, consider the following:

- If it is not necessary to know your respondent's name, do not ask for it. Anonymous questionnaires are more likely to yield honest answers.
- Provide adequate instructions about how to answer the questions. For example, Alvin's instructions ("rank order how important each date characteristic is *to you*") let respondents know they are being asked for their own opinion, not the opinion they believe to be held by their peer group. However, he should have asked respondents to "rate" rather than "rank order" the characteristics.
- Number each question in the questionnaire. Space questions out on the page so that they are easy to read.
- Be careful about the order in which questions are listed. Put easy questions first and difficult or sensitive questions last.
- Show respect for your respondents. Thank them for their cooperation and retain the confidentiality of their responses.

Again, Alvin's questionnaire incorporates most of these suggestions.

Alternatively, your assignment may allow you to use not only existing measures developed by other researchers, but their data as well. This is called secondary survey analysis. Many large universities subscribe to the quantitative data library service provided by the Interuniversity Consortium for

TABLE 9-1
EXAMPLE OF A SURVEY: QUESTIONNAIRE FOR ALVIN'S PAPER

Questionnaire # _____

Student Dating Questionnaire

The following questionnaire is anonymous. Your answers will be held in the strictest confidence.

Please circle your answers to the following questions.

1. What is your sex?
   a. male
   b. female
2. Do you belong to a university-sponsored fraternity or sorority?
   a. yes   If yes, please specify which one: _____
   b. no

Using the five-point scale (where 1 = not at all important and 5 = extremely important), please rank order how important each date characteristic is *to you*.

	Not at All Important				Extremely Important
3. Physical Attractiveness	1	2	3	4	5
4. Personality	1	2	3	4	5
5. Sense of Humor	1	2	3	4	5
6. Potential Occupational Success	1	2	3	4	5
7. Attitude Similarity	1	2	3	4	5

Please circle your answers to the following questions:

8. Have you dated in the last year (that is, gone out for purely social purposes with the possibility of developing a romantic involvement)?
   a. yes
   b. no
9. If you have dated in the last year, have you dated someone from a fraternity or sorority?
   a. yes   If yes, please specify which fraternity or sorority: _____.
   b. no

Thank you for taking the time to complete this questionnaire. Your cooperation is greatly appreciated!

Political and Social Research (ICPSR). One of the most commonly used data sets provided by the ICPSR is the General Social Survey collected by the National Opinion Research Center (NORC). Check with your instructor about this data library. If ICPSR services your university, and if its use is acceptable for the purposes of your assignment, your task for the methods and analysis plan would involve the selection of an appropriate database, and within that the selection of specific questions to be used in your analysis.

3. **How long will it take to collect the data?** Consult your time grid and our suggestions on managing your time (Chapter 2).

4. **How will you get the data into an analyzable form?** For example, have you assigned an appropriate numerical equivalent (no = 1, yes = 2) to the response scales of closed-ended questions? Have you developed a coding scheme for open-ended questions? For example, your coding scheme could involve counting the number of respondents who made some reference to social mobility in response to an open-ended question, or counting the number of times different types of respondents mentioned themes of alienation. Remember that in a quantitative paper, you must be able to represent all responses numerically.

If you are an advanced student planning on forming an attitude index or scale from a set of closed-ended questions, will the response scores of any of your questions need to be reversed? That is, before adding the response scores of several questions together to form a single scale, will the response scores of negatively worded questions be reversed so as to bring them in the same direction as positively worded questions? Will you leave the index as a continuous variable or will you divide it at the median so as to compare high and low scorers?

5. **How will you analyze the data?** Depending on your hypotheses and the level of statistical knowledge required for your assignment, there are different ways to do this. If you haven't taken statistics, the two simplest ways to analyze your data would be to calculate percentages or averages on each variable, independently of other variables. Independent percentages or averages are often quite adequate for reporting the results of an exploratory study.

However, in testing hypotheses it is often necessary to look at the relationship between two variables. The complexity of calculating percentages or averages increases when you examine the relationship between two variables because the variables must be examined jointly. Some common methods of doing this include constructing a cross-tabulation table (see Tables 1 and 2 in the sample quantitative paper), a table of means (see Table 3 in the sample quantitative paper), and a correlation matrix (not shown). In each type of table, one variable is designated as the row variable and the other as the column variable.

Although constructing a correlation matrix is most feasible for advanced students, beginning students may be able to calculate the cross-tabulation table or table of means (averages). For example, in Table 1 of the sample paper (see p. 175), Alvin uses the prestige ranking of students' fraternities or sororities as the column variable and the prestige ranking of the dates' fraternity or sorority as the row variable. In preparing the table, Alvin first rated the prestige level of the respondents' fraternities or sororities. Then, on the basis of this information, he sorted the questionnaires into three piles (high, medium, and low prestige). *Separately for each pile,* he counted the number of respondents who reported dating a student from a high-, medium-, or low-prestige Greek organization. He repeated this procedure for each pile, producing a set of frequencies to be used in calculating the percentages. Notice at the top of each column in Table 1 that Alvin specifies the number of students from high- ($N = 10$), medium- ($N = 10$), and low-prestige ($N = 10$) Greek organizations. This lets the reader know that the denominator used in calculating the percentages for each pile is 10. For example, Alvin found that out of the 10 high-prestige students, 8 reported dating another high-prestige student ($8 \div 10 = 80\%$) and 1 reported dating a medium-prestige student ($1 \div 10 = 10\%$). At the bottom of each column, Alvin includes the total percentage so that the reader knows how to read the table (for example, $80\% + 10\% + 10\% = 100\%$).

In Table 3 of the sample paper, Alvin calculates averages instead of percentages (see p. 179). He uses student status as the row variable and the five date characteristics as the column variable. Again he designates in parentheses the number of respondents in each status category. In preparing this table, Alvin sorted the questionnaires into four piles (Greek Males, Independent Males, Greek Females, Independent Females) according to the respondents' status. Then, *separately for each pile,* Alvin added together the numerical scores given by every respondent for each date characteristic. He divided each sum by the number of students in the pile. For example, the responses of the 15 Greek males in pile 1 for the date characteristic "physical attractiveness" summed to 66 ($5 + 4 + 4 + 5 + 4 + 5 + 4 + 3 + 5 + 5 + 4 + 5 + 5 + 4 + 4 = 66$). Alvin divided 66 by the number of the respondents in the pile to obtain the average score ($66 \div 15 = 4.4$). Alvin repeated this procedure for each date characteristic.

Try to make a mock table for analyzing and presenting your results. That is, try to specify which variable you will use as your row variable and which variable as your column variable. Which variables will you use to sort respondents into piles? Determine whether the numbers in the cells will be percentages or averages.

If you are required to carry out more sophisticated statistical analyses of your data, determine the level of measurement of your variables (nominal, ordinal, interval, or ratio). This will allow you to decide which statistical tests can be appropriately calculated. Computer software packages that calculate social science statistics are available for microcomputers. Check with your instructor.

Don't proceed with your data collection or analysis until your instructor has approved your methods and analysis plan and answered your questions. Once you complete your data collection and analysis, you are ready to begin writing the other sections of your paper.

WRITING THE OTHER SECTIONS OF YOUR PAPER

THE METHODS SECTION

The methods section directly follows the introduction. It should contain three subparts: sample, measures, and procedure. Each part should be labeled with an italicized heading at the left margin; capitalize only the first letter. (See pp. 171 and 173 of Alvin's paper for examples of these headings.) Begin the methods section by describing your sample.

▶ **Describing Your Sample.** Specify the population studied. Discuss in detail how you selected your sample from this population. Did you randomly select respondents—that is, give every member of the population an equal chance of being included in the sample—or did you select whomever you could get? If respondents were randomly selected, describe the steps you took to ensure randomness (for example, tossing a coin or systematically selecting every fifth residence). If you are a more advanced student, did you stratify your sample on any particular variable?

Describe all the relevant characteristics of your sample (for example, age, sex, race). If you had to eliminate any subjects because of incomplete data or for other reasons, state the number and the reason. Specify the final overall sample size and the size of each group.

▶ **Describing Your Measures.** If you obtained your data from secondary sources, describe where the original data came from and how they were measured. If you did a structured observation, describe the behaviors, types of people, situations, and so on that you observed.

If you used a questionnaire or interview, state whether you used closed-ended or open-ended questions, questions newly developed by you, or questions adapted from previous research. If you used existing scales or indexes, include information about their validity and reliability, if available. "Validity" refers to the extent to which the questions actually measure what they are supposed to measure. "Reliability" refers to the stability of measurements taken at different times.

In the body of the paper, quote the actual question(s) used to operationally define each variable. If several questions were used, as in the construction of an index or a scale, give a sample of the questions and include the others in a table or an appendix. For example, "Gender role attitudes were measured by agreement-disagreement with 20 statements, such as 'The woman's place is in the home' and 'I would vote for a woman presidential candidate' (see Appendix)." If the questions were closed-ended, state the range of the response scale and describe the anchor points. For example, you might state that you used "a five-point Likert response scale ranging from (1) not at all to (5) extremely." If you averaged several questions together to form an index, state what the high and low scores on the index signify. For example, "A high score on the gender role index indicates liberal gender role attitudes; a low score indicates conservative attitudes." If the questions were open-ended, describe the coding scheme that you used to code the data.

▶ **Describing Your Procedure.**   Identify the method you used. Describe when (time of day, day of week, date), where (the geographic location, type of institution, building), and under what circumstances the study took place. This information is especially important if the study was conducted in a field setting.

If you conducted an experiment, be sure to also specify the design. Discuss the procedure by which the independent variable(s) was manipulated and the instructions given to respondents in each group. Specify any additional precautions taken to control extraneous variables or to exclude bias from your sample. For example, did you randomly assign respondents to experimental conditions? (Random assignment to groups is different from random selection.) If you employed confederates (accomplices), describe who they were, what they did, and whether or not they were kept "blind" (ignorant) to the hypotheses.

Whichever method you chose, summarize each step you took in collecting your data. A good rule of thumb is to describe your methods in enough detail that another researcher could replicate your study.

THE RESULTS SECTION

Discuss how you examined the relationship between your variables. Did you count the number of people who gave each type of response, or did you average the scores of several people? If you calculated percentages or took averages, state the number of people used as the denominator in your calculations.

If you have a large amount of data to report, consider displaying it in a table or figure. Put each table or figure on a separate page at the end of the paper, just before the list of references. Each table should be numbered consecutively. The number should end with a period and be followed by an indent and a descriptive title. The line consisting of the table number and descriptive title should be flush with the left margin and made bold, and it should be followed by a double rule (also bold), as shown in Table 9-2. A good title allows the reader to tell what is in the table without having to refer to the text. For figures, the number and descriptive title should

TABLE 9-2
SAMPLE TABLE

Table 1. Gender Role Attitudes by Sex of Respondent

	Sex of Respondent	
Gender Role Attitudes	Male (N = 100)	Female (N = 100)
Liberal	55%	85%
Traditional	45	15
TOTAL	100%	100%

also be flush with the left margin and bold, but they should be positioned below the graph or diagram, as shown in Figure 9-1. Figures should also be numbered consecutively. In the body of the paper, refer to each table or figure by number; then explain it. Remember that the numbers presented in the table never speak for themselves.

Another way to present your results is to use graphs or charts. You can draw these by hand or you can use one of the many computer graphics programs that are available for both mainframe and personal computers. The best known of these programs for the advanced student are SPSS (formally known as the Statistical Package for the Social Sciences) and the SAS (Statistical Analysis System), which can also be used to perform statistical analyses. Programs such as Microsoft's Excel and Corel's QuattroPro can be most useful for the less advanced student. Often visual aids can dramatically illustrate the relationships between variables. Whether you should use a bar chart, a line graph, or a causal model will depend on the type of data that you have and the analyses you perform. Ask your instructor for suggestions on the best way to present your results.

FIGURE 9-1
SAMPLE FIGURE

Figure 1.   Measurement Model of Gender Role Attitudes

If your assignment required statistical analyses, state the statistical tests performed; their critical values, degrees of freedom, and significance levels; and the direction of the results. For example, "The relationship between gender role attitudes and sex of respondent is reported in Table 1. The results of a chi-square test indicate that a significantly greater proportion of females (85%) than males (55%) hold liberal gender role attitudes ($x^2 = 24.24$, d.f. = 100, p < .01)." In the discussion section, you will take this explanation a step further.

THE DISCUSSION SECTION

In the discussion section you should tie your results back in to your hypotheses. Did the data support any of your hypotheses? Remember that the statistical significance of your findings does not indicate the theoretical, substantive, or practical significance of your findings. The latter is a judgment you must make in the discussion section. What does a relationship between X and Y mean in the larger theoretical context? How do your findings compare with previous research? What has the study contributed to the existing body of literature on this topic? What are the practical implications of your findings, if any? What ethical issues were raised?

What is the internal and external validity of your study? That is, to what extent does your study provide an adequate test of your hypotheses? To what other populations can your findings be generalized? Discuss any methodological or design flaws, particularly if your hypotheses are not supported. Make suggestions for improving future research. If the study is methodologically sound, how can you account for your unexpected findings? Do the data support an alternative theory?

What conclusions can you draw? What direction should further research on this topic take?

THE TITLE

Now that you've completed the main sections of your paper, you will be able to come up with a good descriptive title. It should be short (rarely over 12 words) and include the theoretical perspective taken and/or the major variables examined (both independent and dependent, where appropriate). (See Chapter 5 for guidelines on formatting a title page.)

THE ABSTRACT

The abstract, usually about 100–200 words in length, is a very brief summary of your paper. It describes the problem, method, sample, results, and conclusions of your study and should contain only ideas or information already discussed in the body of the paper. The abstract goes on a separate (labeled) page right after the title page. For a heading, type ABSTRACT (in capital letters) and center it. Triple space between the heading and the body of the abstract. Indent the first line. (See p. 167 of the sample paper for an example of an abstract.) Although almost always included in a journal article, an abstract may not be required by your instructor.

THE LIST OF REFERENCES

If no specific journal style is required, follow the guidelines given in Chapter 4 for formatting your list of references. Include in your list only those sources you actually cite in the body of your paper. The list of references should appear on a separate page at the end of your paper (see p. 185 for an example).

THE APPENDIX

The appendix is optional. Some instructors may want you to include your raw data, statistical calculations, questionnaire, observation checklist, instructions to respondents, or other items in an appendix. The appendix, when included, goes after the list of references.

SUGGESTED READINGS

Babbie, Earl R. 1995. *The Practice of Social Research.* 7th ed. Belmont, CA: Wadsworth Publishing Co., Inc.
Bailey, Kenneth D. 1994. *Methods of Social Research.* 4th ed. New York: The Free Press.
Fowler, Floyd J. 1993. *Survey Research Methods.* 2nd ed. Newbury Park, CA: Sage Publications.

A SAMPLE STUDENT PAPER

The following sample quantitative research paper, a study of college student dating patterns, was written by Alvin Hasegawa for an undergraduate course in quantitative research methods. Choosing a date may seem like a personal issue, but Alvin's study and others like it reveal that this individual decision is shaped by such sociological factors as class background and membership in particular organizations—for example, sororities and fraternities.

   Alvin's assignment required him to work in a group with other students to design a study, construct measures, collect data, and tabulate results. However, each student was responsible for writing her or his own report of the research. Alvin's paper, then, is based on a group project. Alvin and his co-workers discussed their methods and analysis plan with the instructor before they collected their data to ensure that they were on the right track.

Alvin reviewed the relevant literature on dating and developed his main thesis to answer questions raised there. The group retested other researchers' hypotheses that dating among Greek students (members of sororities and fraternities) and Independent students is homogamous; that is, that partners are chosen from within the same social group. The student group went beyond other studies by also asking respondents to rank the importance of various characteristics of a dating partner. Thus, this work is located within an ongoing discussion but also contains something original, both of which are important considerations in designing sociological research.

The paper follows a journal article format and is based on quantitative results from a survey. Notice that it is organized into the major sections discussed in this chapter: title page, abstract, introduction (which includes a review of the literature), methods, results, and discussion. Alvin also provides tables that present important results in an easily read format. His list of references appears at the end of the paper. Our comments on the facing pages detail other important features of the paper as well as ways in which it could be improved.

OUR COMMENTS

Because of the length of his paper, Alvin has included a title page (as suggested in Chapter 5).

The title "Dating" is not very descriptive. The title should reflect the major variables being investigated. A more appropriate title would be "Homogamous Dating among Greeks and Independents."

Dating

Alvin Hasegawa
Sociology 109
Professor Giarrusso
May 27, 1992

In the abstract, Alvin provides a brief summary of his paper. He describes the problem, methods, results, and conclusions of his study. He includes only ideas and information discussed in the body of the paper.

ABSTRACT

According to Waller (1937), dating among university
students is based on the "rating-dating complex." However,
other researchers suggest that the dating patterns of
students are more complex and may actually follow the
principle of homogamy. A survey study of university students
was conducted to examine these two theories. A total of 68
students responded to questions about the prestige ranking
of campus Greek organizations, their own dating patterns,
and the importance of five date characteristics. The
responses of male and female Greek (members of fraternities
and sororities) and Independent (non-Greek) students were
compared. The results revealed that the Greek system is
stratified on the basis of prestige and that members of the
Greek system do date in a homogamous manner. In addition, it
was found that the dating patterns of Independents reflect
their social background. Finally, the results revealed that
Greeks and Independents differentially rank the importance
of five date characteristics. It was concluded that student
dating patterns follow the principle of homogamy.

Alvin locates his study in the larger body of literature on marriage and the family. Also, by discussing Waller's classic study, Alvin shows that his research question is rooted in a long-standing sociological tradition.

Alvin uses the phrase "in contrast" as a transition between paragraphs (see Chapter 3).

Here Alvin shows how the positions of Reiss and Krain et al. differ from that of Waller. These studies try to show the limitations of Waller's earlier work. Alvin briefly refers to the theory, hypotheses, methods, and results of these two studies.

Most of us hope that someday we will find that perfect someone whom we will marry. But, in order to accomplish this task, we must go through that courtship system commonly known as the marriage market. Thus, in order to select a mate, we must first go through the dating process. Our group study focused on this aspect of marriage and the family.

In our search for existing data, we came across two important studies. The first was done by Reiss (1965); the second, by Krain, Cannon, and Bagford (1977). Both studies were based upon earlier work done by Waller (1937) on the "rating-dating complex" on college campuses. According to Waller, casual dating among Greeks (members of fraternities and sororities) is a prestige contest based mainly on such factors as having a car, money, and nice clothes, and belonging to the best fraternity/sorority. However, this status-seeking pattern isn't true for seriously dating couples whose goal is mate selection.

Reiss (1965), in contrast to Waller, hypothesized that the Greek class system and related dating actually reflect parental class background. This pattern of dating supports the principle of homogamy because it encourages marriage among those who are similar in social background. To test this hypothesis, Reiss used two surveys: one to rank the Greek organizations and a second to obtain information on Greek dating patterns. He found that most of those in high-ranking Greek organizations had fathers in high occupations (executives, etc.). This was less true in the low-ranking Greek organizations. In the second part of his study, he found that high-ranking Greeks tended to date other high-ranking Greeks, whereas low-ranking Greeks dated elsewhere. This finding supported his hypothesis and showed how parents unintentionally achieve homogamy.

Krain et al. (1977) hypothesized that "stratified prestige structures [do] exist to differentiate Greek organizations from each other" (p. 666). They also believed that dating would tend to be confined within the levels of such structures. Unlike Waller, however, they assumed that serious as well as casual dating would reflect prestige homogamy. With this, they developed two surveys: one on

A review of three studies is not "thorough." Alvin should either acknowledge that the review was very selective or state that there were few studies conducted on this topic (which, in this case, is not true).

Here, Alvin states three hypotheses, clearly and in a way that can be unambiguously confirmed or rejected.

Here Alvin introduces some new questions.

"Replication" means more than just using the same method. Alvin should have specified exactly how his study is the same.

How many of each group? How many of each sex? What age range? Were students given self-administered questionnaires or face-to-face interviews?

Alvin includes both questionnaires in an Appendix (only one of which is reproduced in this book, however, for the sake of brevity).

perceptions of Greek organizations' prestige and a second
on dating patterns among those with Greek affiliation. They
found support for both of their hypotheses in the analysis
of their results.

    After a thorough review of the literature, we decided to
retest the hypotheses formulated by these earlier
researchers. Our first two hypotheses dealt with the Greek
system here at UCLA. Based on Krain et al.'s (1977) study,
our first hypothesis was that Greek systems will be
stratified in terms of hierarchical prestige ratings. Our
second hypothesis was that those in the Greek system will
tend to date in a homogamous manner based on the prestige
ranking of their Greek organizations. Our third hypothesis
tied in with Reiss's (1965) work, but instead of dealing
with Greeks, it concerned "Independents"—non-Greek UCLA
students. Thus, our third hypothesis was that parental
class background will be reflected in the dating patterns
of Independents. Finally, we decided to ask some questions
not included in either of the above studies on the rank-
order importance of five characteristics in a dating
partner. Since we did not have any hypotheses about these
characteristics, these questions were just exploratory.

                              METHOD

Design
    Because we chose to use hypotheses previously tested, we
simply replicated the research design; that is, we used the
survey method.

Sample
    We surveyed a total of 68 students from two separate
groups: Greeks and Independents.

Measures
    We constructed two different survey instruments (see
Appendix). The first would be used to place the Greek
organizations into ranks, according to prestige. The second

Because the word "data" is plural, not singular, the verb should also be plural: "The data were. . . ."

Anyone? How were the subjects selected? This section is very weak. Alvin should have given enough detail for another researcher to replicate his study.

Here Alvin tries to control for bias in the data analysis.

Where are the data? He should have included them in a table.

survey would be used to measure, for both Greeks and
Independents, demographic information, dating patterns, and
the rank-order importance of five characteristics in a
dating partner.

Procedure

After completing the surveys the next step was to
collect the data. The data was collected over the weekend
of April 25, 1992. The first survey, which asked students
to rank-order the various Greek houses on campus, was given
to anyone who had knowledge about the fraternities and
sororities. This survey was given to 15 Greek individuals.
Our second survey, measuring dating patterns and the
importance of the five characteristics, was administered to
both Greeks and Independents. This survey was given to 30
Greeks (15 males and 15 females) and 23 Independents (15
males and 8 females). The Greek participants were surveyed
at their respective houses, while the Independents were
surveyed at the dormitories.

RESULTS

In analyzing our first survey, student rankings of his/her
own organization were excluded from the results in order to
control for partiality toward one's own Greek organization.
We found that the Greek system was indeed stratified, as our
data showed a clear-cut view of the separate classes. Each
house fell neatly into one of three categories: high, medium,
or low. There seemed to be a consensus as to which houses
were at the top and which were not.

Our second survey on homogamous dating patterns had to
be analyzed separately for Greeks and Independents, owing
to the different criteria on which prestige was based for
each group.

In our analysis of Greeks, we used the results of the
first survey to divide students (based on their Greek
membership) into high, medium, or low prestige. Of the 30
Greeks surveyed, an equal number of males and females (5
each) came from high-, medium-, and low-ranking

Alvin refers the reader to the table, then explains what the numbers in the table mean.

Where are the data on sex differences? Again, Alvin should have included these in a table.

Unless your instructor says otherwise, each table should go on a separate page at the end of your paper, just before the references, rather than in the body of the paper.

This is a well-prepared table. In order to test his hypothesis, Alvin cross-tabulates two nominal level variables to examine their relationship.

Alvin details exactly how social class was calculated and refers to the source of this formula. However, the questionnaire he turned in with his paper does not include the questions on father's occupation and education. He should have included them.

The cutoff point used to divide subjects into categories is specified.

fraternities and sororities. The results are reported in
Table 1. We found that Greeks in the high-prestige
organizations tended to date other high-prestige Greeks.
Those Greeks in the medium-prestige range dated both within
their own category and with those in higher categories. For
those in the low-prestige organizations, our results showed
that they dated within their own category. These findings
were characteristic of both males and females in the Greek
system. We also noted that women in high-prestige
categories did not date any less-prestigious Greeks, and
the low-prestige men did not date any higher-ranked Greeks.

Table 1. Prestige Ranking of Member's Greek Organization
          by Prestige Ranking of Date's Greek Organization

		Prestige of Member's Greek Organization		
		H (N = 10)	M (N = 10)	L (N = 10)
Prestige of	High	80%	40%	10%
Date's Greek	Medium	10	50	20
Organization	Low	10	10	70
	TOTAL	100%	100%	100%

    Next, we had to analyze the data from our Independent
subjects. In order to get prestige rankings for students in
this group, we used a measure that reflected parental class
background. There were two questions on the survey that
inquired about their father's occupation and education.
Using this information and a social class rating formula,
we could determine social class ratings. The formula was:

    (Occupational Rating × 7) + (Educational Rating × 4) =
    Social Class Rating.

(See King and Ziegler, 1975, for a description of this
formula.) We decided that any score of 60 and above would rank
in the upper-class/high-prestige category. Anything below 60
would fall into the lower-class/low-prestige category.

It was a good decision to analyze the data separately for males and females, since the females were all upper class.

This type of statement relating the size of the group to the conclusion should go in the discussion section, not in the results section.

Table 2 also gives a good presentation of the results. The column and row variables of the table are clearly labeled and a descriptive title is provided. For each row, the size of each group is specified in parentheses and the total percent is included so the reader will know how the table should be read.

Subjects may have found the response categories 1 to 5 confusing since they were asked to rank (rather than rate) each characteristic.

Of the eight female Independents, none fell into the
lower- or middle-class category. However, in classifying
the male Independents, we were able to separate them into
upper and lower classes. Therefore, we decided to analyze
the results separately for male and female Independents.

Table 2 shows that 50 percent of the female Independents
date Independent or off-campus males (that is,
nonstudents), although our hypothesis would have predicted
a similar number dating Greeks (since the females are of
high social class). However, because of the very small
sample size, these results are inconclusive.

Table 2. Prestige Ranking of Independent Females and Males
         by Prestige of Date

Prestige Ranking of Independents	Prestige of Date			
	Greeks	Independent/ Off-Campus	Don't Date	TOTAL
Upper-Class Females (N = 8)	25%	50%	25%	100%
Upper-Class Males (N = 9)	56	33	11	100
Lower-Class Males (N = 6)	0	50	56	100

We also see from Table 2 that a large number of male
Independents date both Greek and Independent females in the
upper-class category. In the lower class, note that none of
the Independent males date Greek females, and half of them
do not date at all.

Finally, we analyzed the results of the rank-ordering of
the five characteristics in a dating partner. We did the
analysis separately for males and females, Greeks and
Independents. Subjects ranked each characteristic on a five-
point scale from "(1) not at all important" to "(5)
extremely important." In Table 3 we show the average ranking
of each characteristic, for each subgroup. We can see that
the scores for all five characteristics for females, whether

Alvin constructs a table of means to determine whether any differences exist between males and females or Greeks and Independents in terms of the importance of various characteristics of a date.

Again, the verb should be "were," not "was."

Greek or not, are the same. Both Greek and Independent
females ranked personality as most important, and potential
occupational success as second most important. For the
males, the results are quite different depending on their
Greek affiliation. Greek males rated physical attractiveness
as the most important characteristic, whereas the
Independent males thought personality was the most
important. Physical attractiveness came in third, after a
sense of humor, for male Independents.

Table 3. Average Rankings of Five Characteristics by Male
         and Female Greeks and Independents

	Physical Attrac- tiveness	Person- ality	Sense of Humor	Potential Occupational Success	Attitude Similar- ity
Greek Males (N = 15)	4.4	3.8	2.9	1.4	2.4
Independent Males (N = 17)	2.6	3.8	2.9	1.3	2.4
Greek Females (N = 15)	2.8	4.2	2.5	3.1	2.3
Independent Females (N = 8)	2.4	3.3	1.9	2.5	2.0

DISCUSSION

   Now that all the data was analyzed, we reviewed our
hypotheses. Our first hypothesis, that the Greek system
would be stratified according to prestige, was supported by
our first survey. It showed a consensus of opinion about

In the discussion section, Alvin reintroduces his hypotheses and states whether they were supported.

Here Alvin offers an interpretation of the results. He introduces the concept of self-esteem and shows how this concept can explain his findings.

This effective transitional sentence reminds the reader what the paper has already addressed and summarizes what's coming next (although all transitional sentences do not have to follow this pattern).

Alvin went beyond replication by bringing in a new set of questions. However, he should have gone further in interpreting the findings.

Here Alvin makes a concluding statement. He relates his findings to previous research and notes the contribution of his study. Note one small, but common, error: although "data" is a plural noun, Alvin uses the singular "has" as its verb. The phrase should read, ". . . and the data *have* been consistent with previous findings."

which houses belong to high-, medium-, or low-prestige
categories. Our second hypothesis stated that Greeks would
tend to date in a homogamous manner. This, too, was
supported. We saw, in general, that high-prestige Greeks
date other high-prestige Greeks. The Greeks in low-prestige
categories also date each other.

The fact that the medium-prestige Greeks dated both high
and medium Greeks may at first be deceptive. But it too
supports our second hypothesis. Those who dated from medium
to high may have had high self-esteem and perceived
themselves as dating a Greek of similar status.

Our third hypothesis was that the dating patterns of
Independents would reflect their social class background.
Since we assumed that Greek organizations have prestige, we
expected to find that upper-class Independents would date
as many Greeks as Independents, and that lower-class
Independents would stay away from Greeks. Our results seem
to have confirmed this hypothesis. We found that upper-
class Independents were able to date Greeks just as
frequently as they did Independents. And we found that the
lower-class Independents did not date Greeks at all; they
stayed with the Independents or did not date.

In addition to the three hypotheses we tested for, we
had subjects rank five characteristics of a date in order
of their importance. Although we had no clear hypotheses as
to what we could expect, the results were interesting. It
is interesting to note, for example, that "potential
occupational success" was ranked second in importance by
all females. This may imply a female's need for security
and a belief in the traditional role of male support. The
results for the males' ranking of the importance of
physical attractiveness were similar to the females. The
Greek males rated it as the most important characteristic.
Are Greek guys really only interested in a girl's body?

All in all, our results seem to have supported our
hypotheses, and the data has been consistent with previous
findings. Although our research model paralleled others,
our study did add to the previous studies by applying
earlier concepts to a new sample, and by comparing how

Although this paragraph highlights the importance of managing your time, it is irrelevant to Alvin's discussion of his study's weaknesses. Alvin's critique should be directed toward the limitations of his methodology.

Alvin should have put quotation marks around the words "casual" and "serious" to indicate to the reader that these were the actual words used in the questionnaire.

This is a common mistake made by students. In scientific communication, "random" means something more than what we mean in everyday language. Alvin also seems to have misunderstood that it is the selection process, not the sample size, that determines the representativeness of the sample.

It is important to be aware of any ethical problems with your study before you undertake data collection. Alvin shows that he was sensitive to this issue.

At the polishing stage, Alvin should have revised to avoid four "he or she" phrases in close proximity. See Chapter 5 for further explanation.

Unless your assignment requires some discussion of the group processes experienced while undertaking your research project, this type of information should not be included. Also, the informality of the last sentence is inappropriate for scientific communication.

Alvin should have ended his paper by suggesting a direction for future research.

Greek and Independent males and females rank-order the importance of characteristics in a date. However, this is not to imply that there were no problems with our research. Nothing could be less true.

Time is a limited resource, and for our group, it was very precious. Although we had ideas in our heads as much as three weeks in advance, it wasn't until a week before our presentation that we got them down on paper. That, perhaps, was our major downfall, but not our only one.

The survey itself was not perfect. It contained oddly worded questions and vague ideas. A few questions could have been reworded in order to prevent confusion. In particular, we might have operationally defined some terms such as casual or serious dates. Finally, our last question should have read "rate" instead of "rank." This minor detail could have made a major difference in our results.

Another problem related to the survey was our sample population. With only 56 subjects in all, our results could not have been highly representative. And, although our subjects were chosen at random, it was not completely random. Since we sampled residents of only one floor of the dorm, the results may only reflect the attitudes of students on that floor and not the entire UCLA population.

As far as ethics are concerned, this research was pretty fair. Our surveys were anonymous, so no one would feel as if they were giving up intimate secrets for everyone to see. The only ethical issue that might arise would be if a subject discovered that he or she was in a low-prestige ranking or if he or she found out that he or she did not date. Of course, the subject knows whether he or she dates, but the survey may rub it in. The realization that one does not date may result in lowering self-esteem.

In conclusion, our group made up for our problems with our effort. Although we could have (and should have) started earlier, we didn't. But that didn't stop us. We all worked hard and with cooperation we finished our project fairly successfully. Now that we're through, we can all relax, and go out and find some dates.

Alvin includes in his list of references only the sources he actually cites in his paper. However, he should have included more current references on the topic. He correctly follows the format recommended in Chapter 4.

REFERENCES

King, Michael and Michael Ziegler. 1975. *Research Projects in Social Psychology: An Introduction to Methods.* Monterey, CA: Brooks/Cole Publishing Co.

Krain, Mark, Drew Cannon, and Jeffery Bagford. 1977. "Rating-Dating or Simply Prestige Homogamy." *Journal of Marriage and the Family* 39:663-674.

Reiss, Ira L. 1965. "Social Class and Campus Dating." *Social Problems* 13(2):193-205.

Waller, Willard. 1937. "The Rating-Dating Complex." *American Sociological Review* 2:727-735.

PART THREE
FINISHING UP

A FINAL CHECKLIST FOR SUBMITTING YOUR PAPER

1. Can you quickly identify your thesis—that is, your central argument?

2. Does your thesis remain evident and central throughout the paper?

3. Do you support your thesis with adequate evidence? One trick for checking the quantity and quality of your evidence is to put a mark in the margin of a rough draft wherever you see evidence for your thesis, pausing at each point to review its validity. Instructors sometimes use this method when evaluating the soundness of an argument.

4. Is there a clear, logical relationship among all the paragraphs? If one is irrelevant to your thesis—no matter how dazzling—delete it; if one wanders from the topic, bring it back into line. Stick to the subject.

5. Repeat 4 (above), substituting "sentences" for "paragraphs."

6. Does the writing flow back and forth between generalizations and specifics that support and clarify those generalizations?

7. Are there transitions between paragraphs? Sometimes transitions seem to create themselves naturally during the writing process. Other times you have to create them, very deliberately, at the polishing stage. But make them look natural, not slapped on. The smoothest transitions, perhaps, come in the first sentence of each paragraph, deftly referring back from where you came and forward to where you are going. Your reader will be grateful for transitions because the ride through the paper will be smooth, not bumpy.

8. Now pay attention to transitions between sentences.

9. Do all your words mean what you think they mean? For those occasional moments of doubt, we recommend your owning a good hardcover dictionary (the College Edition of *The American Heritage Dictionary of the English Language* is one good choice) as well as a portable paper-

back if you sometimes write and study in the library. As we mentioned in Chapter 3, be especially careful when using terms that have become part of everyday language and yet retain special sociological definitions (the examples we gave were "stereotype," "status," and "self-fulfilling prophecy"). If you're uncertain about the sociological definitions of your key terms, you might find them quickly in sociology textbooks by using the index and/or glossary. Several dictionaries of sociological terms are also available.

When dealing with words that do not have special sociological meanings, a thesaurus can help you both to locate the most precise word that expresses what you want to say and to find synonyms for varying your word choice. The popular paperback *Roget's College Thesaurus*, in dictionary form, is simple to use because words are alphabetized just as they are in a dictionary. However, before you use a synonym from a thesaurus in your paper, check its meaning in a dictionary. Mark Twain said that "the difference between the almost right word and the right word is really a large matter—'tis the difference between the lightning-bug and the lightning." Believe it or not, the search for "just the right word" can be fun.

10. Have you looked carefully for errors in style (sentence structure, punctuation, spelling, citation)? As we mentioned in Chapter 3, reference books that present style guidelines are available in most bookstores and libraries.

11. What about contractions (for example, "it's," "don't," "you're")? If you do not know your instructor's preference, avoid using contractions.

12. Have you stated your conclusion clearly and forcefully?

13. Have you avoided sexist language (for example, using the masculine pronoun "he" exclusively)?

THINKING BIG

If you or your instructor are particularly pleased with the quality of the paper you produced, you might consider submitting it for presentation at a national or regional meeting of a professional sociological association or for publication in a scholarly journal. Paper presentations and publications, which demonstrate good communication skills, will increase your chance of getting into graduate school and will enhance your résumé.

The main professional organization in sociology is the American Sociological Association (ASA). The ASA holds an annual national meeting for the presentation of both theoretical and empirical research. Usually several sessions are devoted to undergraduate and graduate student papers. The international sociology honor society, Alpha Kappa Delta (AKD), also holds both regional and national meetings in which students have the opportunity to present their work. Ask your instructor or undergraduate counselor for more information about these and other professional associations.

If you wish to submit your paper for publication in a scholarly journal, refer to the list in Chapter 7. Always look inside the jacket of the latest issue of the journal for the name and address of the current editor and the guidelines for submission. Ask your instructor how to draft a cover letter to accompany your paper submission.

REFERENCES TO THE TEXT

Becker, Howard. 1984. *Writing for the Social Sciences*. Chicago: University of Chicago Press.
Durkheim, Emile. [1897] 1951. *Suicide*. Translated by J.A. Spaulding and G. Simpson. Glencoe, IL: Free Press.
Galbraith, John Kenneth. 1979. "Writing, Typing, and Economics." *Atlantic Monthly* (March):102–105.
Mills, C. Wright. 1959. *The Sociological Imagination*. New York: Oxford University Press.
Olson, Gene. 1972. *Sweet Agony*. Grants Pass, OR: Windyridge Press.
Stark, Rodney. 1985. *Sociology*. Belmont, CA: Wadsworth.

INDEX

189

Venn diagrams, describing Boolean
    operators, 68

Web (WWW) sites useful to
    sociologists, 71–72
Word processing, 59–60
Wordiness, 39–40, 43–44
World Wide Web (WWW), 64
Writer's block, 26

Writing
    determining your tasks, 30
    editing, 58–59
    organizing your time (see Time)
    revising, 39–42
    style (see Format)
    typing (see Formatting)
Writing Fieldnotes (Emerson), 130
WWW (World Wide Web), 64